TOM SLICK

MYSTERY HUNTER

For Bud Hampton —
A great explorer and friend!

Catherine

Thomas Baker Slick, Jr.
1916 – 1962

TOM SLICK

MYSTERY HUNTER

Catherine Nixon Cooke

Catherine Nixon Cooke

PARA VIEW

Bracey, Virginia

ISBN: 0-9764986-2-6

Library of Congress Cataloging-in-Publication Data

Cooke, Catherine Nixon, 1950-
Tom Slick, mystery hunter! / Catherine Nixon Cooke.-- 1st Paraview ed.
p. cm.
ISBN 0-9764986-2-6 (9780976498629 : alk. paper)
1. Slick, Tom, 1916-1962. 2. Businessmen--Texas--Biography. 3. Petroleum industry and trade--United States--Biography. 4. Explorers--Texas--Biography. 5. Adventure and adventurers--Texas--Biography. 6. Inventors--Texas--Biography. 7. Philanthropists--Texas--Biography. I. Title.
HD9570.S59C66 2005
338.7'6223382092--dc22

2005025763

First Paraview, Inc. edition 2005

Manufactured in the United States of America

For Betty Slick Moorman,
who asked her big brother to find the ghosts in the attic.
(1917 – 2000)

Contents

Introduction

Where No One Else Has Ever Been

"When you embark for strange places, don't leave any of
yourself safely on shore.
Be brave enough to live life creatively.
The creative place is where no one else has ever been.
You have to leave the city of your comfort and go into the
wilderness of your intuition.
You can't get there by bus, only by hard work and risk ...
...and by not quite knowing what you are doing. .
What you'll discover will be wonderful; what you'll discover
will be yourself."

— Alan Alda

When I heard actor and activist Alan Alda deliver the commencement address at his daughter's college graduation a few years ago, I immediately thought about another graduate, a Phi Beta Kappa at Yale University more than sixty years ago, who lived his life in that wilderness of intuition, never leaving any part of himself "safely on shore". He was a risk taker who traveled to strange places in search of mystery; and Alan Alda was right – what he discovered was wonderful, in the truest sense of the word.

I knew Thomas Baker Slick, Jr., as an uncle; others knew him as a millionaire wildcatter and explorer who drilled for oil and found it, searched for the Yeti in Nepal, spied for the OSS in World War II, discovered diamonds in the Amazon Basin, developed the Brangus breed of cattle and the Liftslab method of construction, established five major research institutes (the first when he was just twenty-five years old), wrote two books on world peace, and died a mysterious death at age forty-six. If it almost sounds like a movie plot, it is; *Tom Slick Monster Hunter* is one of award-winning actor Nicholas Cage's film projects in development. But it's also a true story, with a very complex character at its core. Tom Slick was so much more than a "monster hunter"; *mystery hunter* is a better label if a label is needed, for there was nothing he loved better than an unsolved mystery.

Uncle Tom was a favorite with all children, a Pied Piper cross between a magician and Santa Claus, who understood the importance of playfulness in life. When his spectacular O'Neil Ford-built home was completed in 1960, I was nine years old. I still remember the wonderful housewarming party where guests ranged in age from five or six years old to ninety. One man wore a bright red turban; a glamorous woman wore chiffon and lots of perfume, and was a big topic of conversation at breakfast tables the next day.

A fabulous sunken Japanese tub with fish swimming in it was in my eleven-year-old cousin Patty's bathroom; Uncle Tom told us that someday we would travel to exotic places and learn that there were all sorts of ways to bathe, eat, dress and discover life. Outside, a motorized miniature Model-T Ford circled the driveway, with my ten-year-old cousin Tom at the wheel, his younger brother, Chuck, beside him honking the horn. With a wink, Uncle Tom confided that cars had an uncanny power to attract girls. I've often proven him right in later life.

After a dinner that included some strange courses like snails, and little bowls for dipping fingers, the conversation turned to new research underway at Southwest Foundation and some additions that Uncle Tom had made to his growing art collection. I had never heard of Pablo Picasso, but the grown-ups were duly impressed. As we left the table, he led us down a hallway of contemporary art; our parents helped interpret the paintings for us, pointing out sunsets, ships, and landscapes amidst the colors and shapes. At the end of the hall, Uncle Tom told us that every canvas had been painted by the chimpanzees at Southwest Foundation! He suggested that we should each challenge the meaning of "art". All of the children were delighted; the adults were not as amused.

Like everyone, Tom Slick was shaped by his family situation, his share of disappointments and losses, successes and extraordinary experiences. An early commitment to risk taking, and belief in the intuitive process influenced his life in remarkable ways. His contributions to the twentieth century include breakthroughs in science, agriculture, architecture, and technology, and a long list of unsolved mysteries for us to explore in the next century.

What gave him the courage to listen to his intuition, journey to strange places, and live life creatively, as Alan Alda urged those college graduates to do in 1996? Was it childhood experiences, like the death of his father, when Tom was only fourteen, or the kidnapping of his stepfather by gangster Machine Gun Kelly a few years later? Was it the responsibility created by great wealth to contribute something to the world? Was it an inability to focus on just one thing, requiring large servings of variety and change? Was it the universally human search for "the holy grail," the hero's journey we each follow in our own way? What was the landscape like, in the deep wilderness of his intuition? What complex thoughts and feelings were hidden in the corners of his mind and heart?

He once appeared on a popular television series of the 1950s called "What's My Line," where the audience tried to guess the true identity and accomplishments of each guest on a panel. I was thrilled that my handsome uncle was on television, talking about his expeditions to far-off places in pursuit of mysteries. Nearly fifty years later, his face stares out from the covers of annual reports for the scientific institutes he established; there is a Tom Slick Chair in World Peace at the University of Texas; and actor Nicholas Cage might portray him on film as a "monster hunter," trekking the Himalayas in search of the Yeti. Will the real Tom Slick please stand up?

My discovery of hundreds of letters that Tom Slick wrote between 1948 and 1962, the year he died, filed in stacks of old boxes in a shed at one of his research foundations, provided me with some important clues. As I read them, I climbed into the head of a phenomenal thinker; the process made me wonder if the e-mail correspondence that dominates our communication today will destroy those special insights so unique to letters. Interviews with his ninety-eight-year-old aunt, his sister and brother, his ex-wives, his four children, scientists, secretaries, oilmen, former lovers, and explorers like Sir Edmund Hillary gave me glimpses of a brilliant and complicated man. The "real" Tom Slick remains somewhat of a mystery; but his letters, adventures, and the memories of those who knew him best provide us with some interesting clues and inspiration as we each explore our own mysteries. I think he would like that.

Tom Slick, c. 1938

Chapter One

Ghost Call
April 2001

I *hear birds screeching, followed by the rumble of distant thun-*
der. A thick mist surrounds me and it is very difficult to see. Ice
is falling from the sky like sharp shards of glass; and I am very
cold. I can barely discern a track of some sort, ghostly footsteps in the
snow...I follow.

The dream has come again, both scary and seductive. I zip my
sleeping bag so that just my face is exposed, in a darkness so complete
that the roof of my tent is invisible. I listen. Yes, the thunder is real.

A ghost has lured me to Nepal. For the past two years, his pale
blue eyes have stared at me from a small silver-framed photo; his
correspondence, now yellowed with time, has given me entry to a private world of dreams and visions. Images have haunted me – snowy
mountains, hidden valleys, dark and sacred caves, and mysterious
creatures. I could cannot resist the call to his mythical Shangri-La;
and like everyone who searches for dreams, I believe I might find
answers just over that farthest horizon.

So a group of six friends, boldly calling ourselves "twenty-first-
century explorers," has organized our quest – an expedition to Nepal's
most remote region, where mountain gods still control the rain and
snow, and hidden *beyuls* (valleys) hold the promise of grail-like
discovery. East of Mt. Everest, in the shadow of Mt. Makalu, the
world's fifth highest peak, we have planned to trace the route once
taken by the blue-eyed "ghost" nearly half a century ago. He was
searching for the mysterious Yeti, or Abominable Snowman, whose
legend has inspired expeditions to the tiny Himalayan kingdom for
more than a hundred years. We will not only look for the Yeti, but
also for the ghost of Thomas Baker Slick, Jr., determined to discover

how mysteries guide our life journeys, and why the unknown pulls all of us like a powerful magnet.

Modern explorers like Daniel Taylor and mountaineer Reinhold Messner have made similar searches recently, and their books describe glorious, though difficult, adventures. They say there still are occasional reports of "Yeti sightings", a creature glimpsed crossing the high snow-capped ridges or roaming the isolated thick forests of the Arun Valley. Messner has decided it's a chemo, a member of the bear family; Taylor still thinks that a new species might exist in these mountain ranges, as do Peter Mattheissen and George Schaller. Despite the skepticism of most scientists, the mystery and possibility of the Yeti endure.

We have brought expensive night vision equipment – infrared binoculars and cameras – and state-of-the-art satellite maps have helped us chart our course over a terrain where there are virtually no existing trails and very few inhabitants. We have *not* brought along any communication equipment – no satellite cell phone, no laptop powered by a portable generator, not even a radio. For the next three weeks, we will be in a faraway world, unable to hear the news and noises of our western lives, experiencing a frontier of mystery the way Tom Slick did so many years ago.

When Tom Slick first journeyed to Nepal in 1956, he was forty years old, prematurely silver-haired, with a legendary twinkle in his blue eyes. His body was lean and fit for an entrepreneurial oilman who traveled often and enjoyed fine food and entertaining. But aside from a rather luxurious African safari in 1952, where the guests stayed in large canvas tents with comfortable beds and beautiful rugs, and a number of men's hunting and fishing trips, Slick's outdoor camping experiences were few. He had gathered an impressive expedition team for his search for the Yeti, including a well-respected big game hunter and adventurer named Peter Byrne, and Nepalese porters who found the steep ridges and dense forests as familiar and comfortable as a westerner's "walk in the park."

We have done the same. Our expedition members all are fit by western standards, but no one has climbed much above sixteen thousand feet before; and the thought of no bath for three weeks is a novel idea. Can we endure the physical challenges; will two months of endurance training be enough for the constant ups and downs of peaks and *beyuls* in the little explored Upper Arun Valley? Can we put aside our western mindsets to look for the serenity and magic that might await us in the Himalayas? Will there be any evidence of the Yeti, the elusive creature that drew Tom Slick to the Himalayas three times in the late 1950s? And finally, what will Slick's "ghost" reveal to us about himself, and the many hidden mysteries that wait for us just beyond the ranges?

With a special expedition flag awarded to our group by The Explorers Club, the international organization established in 1904 to promote exploration and scientific contribution all over the world, expert route planning by Scott Hamilton, whose medical expeditions to Mt. Everest have yielded valuable data about the effect of high altitude on our bodies, and Bibhuti Chand Thakur, manager of Himalayan Holidays Trekking in Kathmandu, we feel "official." Our confidence is boosted further by Rabi Thapa and Ram Sharan Thapaliya, two guides who have visited the Arun Valley once before, more than twenty-five porters, the latest in hiking boots and expedition clothing, cameras, and of course, our excitement.

Three of the team members belong to The Explorers Club: Brian Hanson and I serve on the organization's Board of Directors, and twenty-eight-year-old Rima Lewis is a new member of the Club, with a brand new law degree and training in mountain rescue. Dan Bennett is CEO of Sunbelt Sportswear, a large international women's sportswear mail order business; he has researched trekking equipment and brought along the very best, including a water filter system that will prove very valuable. Dr. Brad Towne is a physical anthropologist, an associate professor at the Lifespan Health Research Center at Wright State University Medical School and an associate scientist at Southwest Foundation for Biomedical Research, a research institute founded by Tom Slick in 1948. He has done previous research in Nepal and is familiar with primate behavior and Yeti legends. And finally, Susan Taylor Rosepink, a television journalist, and my best friend, has joined our team, leaving behind a busy career and family life for this adventure. A terrible chest cold has almost prevented her participation; her physician finally gave in to her sheer determination, equipping her with a small pharmacy for the adventure.

The sound of the big Russian helicopter is amazing, first affecting our ears and eventually moving through every part of our bodies. We reach for our earplugs and grip the narrow metal benches as the chopper lifts off, leaving dusty Kathmandu behind. Our backs to the windows, we face a huge pile of duffel bags and equipment in the middle of the helicopter's floor, turning uncomfortably to look out the small plexiglass windows. Soon we've climbed to nine thousand feet and are skirting the foothills of the Himalayas. Nepal has the most dramatic elevation changes in the world – from nearly sea-level in the south, to the towering peaks of Mt. Everest, Kanchenjunga, Lhotse, Makalu, and Chamlang, ranging from twenty-nine thousand to just over twenty-four thousand feet high, respectively. As we bounce over air pockets, heading northeast, incapable of talking over the noise, each team member thinks about the days ahead. I remember my dreams of the ice storm; but the bright blue sky and sunshine soon chase those thoughts away.

After an hour of flight, Rabi enters the cockpit to talk to the morose Russian pilot. It turns out he has never flown to NagiTar before, and is not quite sure where to land. It is a tiny village, just above Tamku at sixty-five thousand feet; far enough from the populated Everest region that the villagers have never seen a helicopter. We touch down in a different world.

Ram is waiting on the ground with about twenty-five porters and a nurse practitioner named Paru. They have walked four days from Tumlingtar, where there is a tiny airstrip, carrying all of the tents, food, and kitchen equipment; and our camp is already set up in the flat meadow just below NagiTar.

Before lunch we hike to the small monastery that is nestled in terraced fields of potatoes, wheat, and mustard, surrounded by neat wooden compounds where fewer than a hundred people comprise the population of NagiTar. It is a steep climb, but not very far. However, I'm aware that this easy thirty-minute journey has challenged my breathing, and I imagine what might be ahead in the days to come. When I reach the top, I smile at Susan, who also is panting just a little bit. She tells me I have blood on my teeth, and I discover I am having a nosebleed ... not an auspicious start.

Descending through the green terraced fields, I'm struck by the spectacular beauty that surrounds us. Past journeys to the turquoise waters of the Mediterranean, the lush jungles of Africa, the white and craggy cliffs of England, the burnt orange desert of the American southwest, and the dense green rice paddies of Indonesia, have all touched that part deep within me, overwhelmed me with their visual and spiritual power. But these mountains in the distance, with their snowy peaks hidden by mist, and these pristine valleys where gentle-eyed Nepalis look at us with curious eyes, create a physical reaction in me that comes as waves of awe, and wonder, and yes, some fear.

Later, after dark and after dinner, we sit around a kerosene lamp and wait for our first visitor from the past, a sixty-three-year-old porter who accompanied Tom Slick on his expeditions in 1957 and 1958. Dawa Tshering Sherpa has walked for about forty-five minutes without light of any kind, barefoot and wearing a light jacket. Ghost-like, he appears at the entrance of the dining tent, just slightly over five feet tall, weighing less than one hundred pounds, and still very strong. He accepts a cup of tea and lets his memories speak.

It was a long time ago. I am an old man now and most of my friends have died. But I am living longer because I am small in stature. I am very strong – it was my job on the Slick Expedition to carry the tents. They were much heavier than the tents you have now because they were made of canvas.

We were looking for the Yeti near a waterfall close to the village of Wallung, where you will go in a few days. Some of the expedition members also wanted to find a Bankati ("wild woman" or "forest girl") that everyone knew lived there, but they couldn't find her. Instead they captured a baby bear.

There are no Bankatis close to NagiTar, but there still are some on the other side of Sedua, a few ridges over that way, where you will also go. Bankatis are very wild; they have very long breasts, which they flip over their shoulders when they run. They turn over rocks and eat frogs. I have never seen a Bankati, but I have seen the frog remains that they leave on the rocks in the forest. And I have heard the sounds they make.

Heeeeeeee.............heeeeeee!

An eerie high-pitched wail echoes in the quiet darkness, and the young porters from our expedition gather around the tent, wide-eyed, to listen to the old man. He tells us about the strange hunting dogs that the Slick Expedition brought to Nepal, imitating their howls, and admits that he ran away from the camp rather than following his orders to kill a goat, something that a Buddhist could not do. He does not read or tell time, but he wears a watch that his son has sent him from India; and around 9:00 p.m., without even stars to guide him, he starts his walk home in total darkness.

The next morning, the trek begins. The next days are spent walking up steep ridges, often at a 75–80 degree angle, for hours, then descending rocky slopes, without a trail, for hours. Soon, all semblance of civilization (for that is now how we remember tiny NagiTar) has disappeared and we are chopping our way through bamboo forests, bushwacking, heading towards the distant Mt. Makalu, which is now hidden by the mist and rain that will become our constant companions.

The next week is spent feeling wet, cold, and tired; our team usually struggles into camp at nightfall, having walked anywhere from six to eleven hours. The physical challenges are occasionally forgotten as we glimpse sacred chortens, draped with prayer flags, on the top of seemingly untravelled ridges, and giant rhododendron trees, more than thirty feet tall, bursting with scarlet blooms. Every day is filled with suffering and redemption.

Towards the end of our first week of trekking, we camp at Rat Mate, which is actually just a small flat clearing where our tents are erected, almost touching, with two *goths*, wooden sheds used to protect herders and their yaks during the winter months. The porters have lit fires in the *goths*, using one for our kitchen, and the other for their shelter; soon drumming and singing join the sound of thunder. As a deluge of rain pounds our tents, we hear a Nepali "concert" a few feet away. It is better than a five-star hotel.

More long days of exhausting ups and downs, made more difficult by the extreme weather, make us wonder if the mountain gods are displeased with us. The rain continues, and at altitudes about eleven thousand feet we encounter snow. Up and down. Up and down. Where is the Yeti? Where is Tom Slick?

At last we arrive in Dobatok, the halfway point of our journey. It is a virtual metropolis, with six tiny homes and a beautiful prayer wheel. Again, we squeeze our tents onto a small bit of empty flat land; and we prepare for our trek to the sacred Khempallung Cave the next day.

The Khempallung Cave is one of the legendary holy places that are said to have been hidden by Guru Rinpoche in the Himalayas centuries ago. It is particularly worshipped by Sherpa, Rai, Khumbo, Shingsapa and Tibetans of Kharte and Dingri. In her chapter in *Mandala and Landscape*, researcher Hildegard Diemberger describes the slopes of the *beyul* ("hidden valley") where the cave is located as "covered with thick forest, inhabited by wild animals, and surmounted by the white Himalayan peaks … in the *beyul* lives the snow lion, the plants know no seasons, there are fruits and flowers and many streams, there is a poisonous burning lake, there are medicinal springs, clouds and mists darken the whole atmosphere, there is a lot of rain; and from the sky you hear the roar of the dragon (thunder)."

During the past days, we certainly have heard the dragon and felt the rain, seen the clouds and mist, been amazed by the plants and flowers blooming almost magically from towering trees, and glimpsed the white peaks during brief moments of clear weather. Tired and more than a little giddy, I am sure the poisonous burning lake will be just around the next bend.

But our climb to the cave proves uneventful; and we are greeted by more than 100 once-colorful prayer flags waving in a blur of faded red, green, blue, yellow and white. They surround a simple stone structure with aluminum siding and wooden benches, where we remove our hiking boots and anything else made of leather. Rabi and Ram invite us to say a prayer and light a butter lamp before moving outside to wash our feet in a sacred waterfall. We move down a rocky slope, painfully since we are barefoot, to the entrance of the cave that Tom Slick described as an oracle. Perhaps his ghost will be waiting inside.

Just inside the rock ledge, there are paintings of the ancient Tara, the feminine goddess said to watch over the cave, as well as a rusted trident and bell. The trident represents the masculine; the bell is symbolic of the feminine; and both are revered in this holy place. Despite the warnings we'd read in academic journals that the cave is not for anyone claustrophobic or plump, I'm astonished at the smallness of the opening and I wonder if any of our larger western bodies will have difficulty passing through the narrow chambers. With our head lamps turned on, we crawl into a dark, very tight space.

Most of the journey is spent either moving along on all fours, or slithering like a snake – using just the arms to pull the body along. Occasionally, we reach a chamber big enough to achieve a sitting position, and there is always a stone Buddha figure or other carved deity to greet us there. One can leave a coin or butter lamp or some other offering, along with a prayer for health, wealth, fertility, abundant crops, or whatever blessing one hopes for.

We reach a particularly tight passage that is called the Purification Chamber, where pilgrims must slide through a narrow, tube-like passageway, circling a rock column clockwise. At one point, when my body is in the shape of the letter "C", panic seizes me. I remind myself that I have come halfway around the world for this experience; I say my *mantra* softly to myself; I am calmer. I begin to slither along the rocky path; suddenly, the idea that I might be stuck overtakes me. I nearly scream, recognizing that I cannot stand up – I can't even sit up or raise my head! I feel myself sinking into a darkness far more frightening than the cave's blackness... then the tiny hand of the Nepalese girl who has gone through the Purification Chamber just ahead of me reaches back to touch mine. I slither on.

I pull out of the c-shaped tunnel, and hear the other team members decide not to pass that way. Later, after we've left the cave, Susan tells me that a huge spider had been overhead, just inches from me, during my entire "purification" effort.

We move further into the cave, crossing a cold, shallow stream that is somehow comforting because it takes my mind off the narrow walls that confine me. The entire traverse takes forty-five minutes, forever; and I crawl into daylight with a renewed sense of life's gifts. According to Buddhist texts, three trips through the Khempallung Cave will bring a pilgrim sainthood. One-third saint is enough for me.

Leaving the hidden valley behind, our journey to Wallung the next day is one of the hardest on the trek. We walk all morning in heavy rain; and the porters are having real trouble because there is no trail to follow. We are bushwacking through thick forest and bad weather. By lunchtime, we realize that we have not made enough progress to reach Wallung by nightfall; everyone is cold, and wet, and miserable. *Na ram-ra* ("not good") becomes a chant from the porters; we agree.

Up a ridge, down to a valley, there is much slipping and falling; and a horrible discovery that we are not alone. When I stop on a flat stretch of soggy ground, removing my backpack to find an energy bar, shedding my rain jacket for a moment, I cause a panic within our group. I look as if I've been shot by a machine gun, with blood splatters all over my t-shirt, places where leeches have attached under the warm band created by my backpack strap. We remove them by lighting matches, shivering, realizing there will be more as we struggle towards Wallung.

By the time we approach the village, it is dark; villagers come up the trail with flashlights to help us over the rocky slope to a small schoolhouse. Instead of going to our wet and leech-infested tents, we decide to sleep on top of the tables in the schoolroom, warm and dry in our sleeping bags. After removing more leeches, spooked by their bloodlust, we are exhausted. We agree that this day has been too much for us; we're not sure we can endure another one like it.

Apparently our porters feel the same way – one says the day has been harder than the trek from Makalu Base Camp to Everest Base Camp; others threaten to quit and go home.

We awaken to sounds of a loud argument between Rabi and the porters, who say the route is too difficult, especially with the terrible rain. Rabi redesigns the route; instead of going all the way to Sedua, we will take a shorter but steeper trek to Norbugaon; and he agrees to pay the porters more to continue.

After crossing two very steep ridges, at times clinging to the face of the mountain, we wonder what the more difficult day would have been like. Finally we arrive in Norbugaon around five thirty, after just slightly more than eight hours of trekking. After de-leeching ourselves and unpacking our sleeping bags, we are almost too tired to eat dinner. Susan's chest cold has worsened; and Rima begins to feel sick at her stomach and excuses herself during the meal. Suddenly a strange woman appears in the doorway of the dining tent.

She screams and seems to be possessed by some unhappy spirit; dancing in a trance, whirling, shrieking. Rabi and Ram usher her away. Everyone goes to bed uneasy; this is not a peaceful place.

Again, we are picking off leeches as we trek over a high ridge in the pouring rain, creating a trail where none exists; and after six hours we arrive in Tashigaon. It is the first real village we've seen in weeks, the place where trekkers and climbers begin the Makalu route that takes them over Shipton Pass to Base Camp and on to the summit of the world's fifth highest mountain. There is a small general store, and an "inn" with two bedrooms.

Some of us opt to sleep in the bedrooms, which each have four wooden cots where we place our sleeping bags; others prefer their tents outside. Just before we blow out the candle that lights the room, Paru removes a huge spider from just above my bed. Being Hindu, she cannot kill it, so she captures it with a kleenex and gently takes it outside. I take a Tylenol PM ... why are these spiders pursuing me?

The next morning, as I wash my face in the small aluminum bowl of hot water, I realize that I've come to consider this a luxury of the day. It startles me when Susan announces that there are only four more days left in our journey; just across snow-covered Shipton Pass, a helicopter will come for us soon.

The trek to Khongma is nearly all uphill, going from about seven thousand five hundred feet to twelve thousand feet. For the most part, I feel strong and enjoy the workout, glad that we're going up, since going down has become increasingly painful for my knees. After about five hours of steady uphill, we encounter a terrible surprise. A freak ice storm, fast, furious and very painful, attacks us. It is my dream, my nightmare, come true.

The slope is very slippery, of course, and to see where to go next, we must look up into shards of falling ice. I stop under a rock shelf to add another layer of clothes from my backpack, but I am already soaking wet and my fingers are too numb to work the zipper. No one is talking; we need every bit of breath and concentration to keep going. The mood is very serious as some of the porters turn back towards Tashigaon, others remove their rubber shoes because they are slipping too much in the snow, and walk barefoot.

Around three thirty in the afternoon, we nearly crawl into Khongma, which is just a flat shelf of snow, with one small aluminum hut with a kerosene stove, where a lady is making tea. Nearly fifty years ago, Tom Slick camped on this same flat shelf, and looked out at a brilliant blue sky and the imposing face of Mt. Makalu in the distance.

We shiver in our wet clothes, drink tea, try to pretend that the kerosene stove emits heat, and pray for a blue sky tomorrow. Susan's cough sounds like pneumonia; the blizzard of snow turns to torrential rain; and the porters finally begin to struggle in with their sixty-pound packs, still barefoot.

Before pitching the tents, they must get warm too. Drums and *raksi*, a strong liquor made from millet, appear in the hut; and soon the body heat of more than twenty people in a tiny space, perhaps twelve feet by twelve feet, creates some warmth. At last, around eight thirty, the final loads arrive. We slip through rain and snow to wet tents, open our wet equipment bags, unpack our wet sleeping bags, and shivering, crawl inside. Everyone is too tired to eat.

The next morning is completely gray, with no visibility because of snow and fog. An Italian expedition team that also has camped at Khongma leaves by 6:00 a.m. for Shipton Pass, wearing crampons and carrying ice axes. Our departure is delayed; Rabi recommends that we stay in Khongma another day, worried about Susan's congestion, Rima's dysentery, and the exhaustion of everyone in the group.

Mid-morning, grim news arrives from higher up the mountain that two climbers have fallen while crossing Shipton Pass. The porter reports that the ridge is especially treacherous. We decide that the high passes ahead – Shipton-La, Tutu-La, and Keke-La – are too challenging with the unexpected snow; wisdom tells us that we are not to be welcomed by the mountain gods this trip. One of our strongest young porters, Dawa Sherpa, is dispatched back down the mountain to Sedua, the nearest village with radio contact. It will be a day's run for him, but would be a journey of several days for us. Dawa will radio our chartered helicopter, instructing it to pick us up in Tashigaon rather than in Yangle Kharka as originally planned.

We spend the rest of the day and the next night in our tents, emerging only for meals, with the wind blowing ferociously. I sleep and listen to my portable walkman, lulled by Fleetwood Mac singer Stevie Nix's mysterious tales of witches and advice to "don't stop thinking about tomorrow." My sleeping bag is finally dry; and I sink in and out of dreams in its cozy warmth. All of us think about real mountain climbers who spend weeks like this, waiting for the weather to clear, hoping to summit their mountain.

The next morning, the mountain gods send us a message of approval. For the first time on the expedition, the day is absolutely clear. There is not a cloud or snowflake or raindrop in the sky. The view of the mountains is incredible…were they really there yesterday, just hidden by the snow and mist?

This is the view Tom Slick saw in 1956, and again in 1958. Not far from this spot, he found a footprint in the snow that he believed belonged to a Yeti. The plaster cast of the print, that he made that day near Khongma, would join his collection of Picassos and other treasures that adorned his home in Texas. The mysteries he had encountered were the same ones we were thinking about as we waited to hear the powerful helicopter blades in the mountain air.

The oracle at Khempallung Cave, the waterfall where the *bankati* still shrieks at night, the footprints we photograph, perhaps of an elusive snow leopard, the leeches and spiders…Tom Slick passed this way first, answering some mysterious call to explore, to search, hopeful that he would discover the creature rumored to be the "missing link" in human evolution. Now, more than forty-five years later, we are on his quest and we find that nothing has changed.

Trekking route through the Arun Valley, climbing towards Mt. Makalu Base Camp, Eastern Nepal.

The Himalayas lured six modern-day mystery hunters to Nepal in 2001, in search of the yeti and the ghost of Tom Slick. View from Rat Mate, Arun Valley, Nepal. (*Photograph by Catherine Nixon Cooke.*)

Left to right, Susan Taylor Rosepink, Brad Towne, Rima Lewis, Dan Bennett, author Catherine Nixon Cooke, and Brian Hanson display the Explorers Club Flag near the base camp of Mount Makalu. (*Photograph by Ram Sharan Thapaliya.*)

Dan Bennett

Catherine Nixon Cooke

Brian Hanson

Rima Lewis

Susan Taylor Rosepink

Brad Towne, Ph.D.

Two porters from Slick's 1958 expedition, near the village of Wallung, still remembered details of the adventure forty-three years later. (*Photograph by Catherine Nixon Cooke.*)

While in the lower altitudes of the Arun Valley (6500 – 9000 feet), thick jungle and frequent rain made the journey difficult. (*Photograph by Brian Hanson.*)

Approaching the tiny village of Wallung, at nearly 9000 feet, the group encountered blood-sucking leeches in the dense forest. (*Photograph by Brian Hanson.*)

17

Trekking guides Ram Sharan Thapaligy and Rabi Thapa were prepared for the almost constant rains at the lower altitides. (*Photograph by Dan Bennett.*)

In the remote village of Dobatok, the trek's halfway point, a local family was still using one of the supply boxes from the Slick expedition to store their grain. (*Photograph by Dan Bennett.*)

Sacred *chortens* decorated by prayer flags were a common site along even the steepest trails, blessing the way. (*Photograph by Catherine Nixon Cooke.*)

The 2001 expedition team encountered snow in the high passes and leeches in the lower jungles, just as Tom Slick had nearly 50 years ago. (*Photograph by Brian Hanson.*)

Not far from this spot above Tashigaon, the porters saw tracks that later turned out to be those of a bear. (*Photograph by Ram Sharan Thapaliya.*)

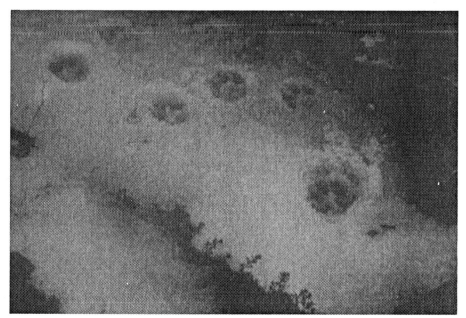

Not far from the tent site at Kongma, the tracks of a clouded leopard were found. (*Photograph by Brian Hanson.*)

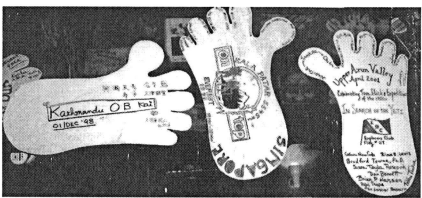

As is the custom in Kathmandu after a yeti expedition, the team left its "footprint" bearing the Explorers Club flag at the famous Ramdoodle Bar. (*Photograph by Susan Taylor Rosepink.*)

Chapter Two

Missing Links

1900–1930

In early May, 1916, the King of the Wildcatters was waiting for two important events. One would occur in an oilfield in Oklahoma, not far from his discovery of huge oil deposits in the Cushing Field in 1912; the other would occur in a hospital in Clarion, Pennsylvania, where his wife of just one year was about to give birth to their first child.

Thomas Baker Slick, Sr., was a workaholic and an explorer; and his discovery of major oilfields in Oklahoma, Texas, and Kansas in the mid-1900s had earned him the nickname of "Lucky Tom" by 1912; and by 1929, he was the largest independent oil operator in the world. As he waited for a new baby and a new oil well, both due the same week, he grappled with priorities, as he always had.

Complex emotions were familiar terrain to Slick, Sr., and his thoughts raced from the almost soothing, practical checklist he followed when drilling a new site, to his wife, nine hundred miles away in Pennsylvania, about to give him a son and namesake. Former oil partner, Bernard B. Jones, had introduced Slick to Berenice Frates just over a year ago; and the couple married almost immediately. The thirty-two-year-old Slick wanted roots; and twenty-five-year-old Berenice Frates, oldest daughter of railroad tycoon Joseph Frates was intelligent, attractive, and understood the wanderlust spirit of her own father, and presumably of the wealthy oilman who was courting her. She was a serious girl, with dark hair and eyes, who had grown up with an incredibly beautiful, vivacious mother, a gregarious, entrepreneurial father, and five younger siblings. As Joseph Frates worked his way up in the railroad business, the family traveled constantly; and Slick believed that his own gypsy spirit would be understood and tolerated by his new in-laws.

Before meeting Berenice in 1915, Slick had recognized that his work habits were not healthy. Following his immense oil discovery in 1912, near Bristow, Oklahoma – the famous "Wheeler Strike" in the Cushing Field – he quickly purchased the majority of leases in the entire area, thanks to a clever scheme. Slick rented every transportation device with miles so no one else could reach the landowners. Exhausted by the intensity and the success, he put his mother (Mary Slick) sister (Flored), and older brother (Jesse) in charge of his business and took an extended trip to Africa and the Orient, exploring China in a rickshaw before returning to Oklahoma in 1913. From rare letters to his family during the trip, it is obvious that Slick was tired and depressed; conditions that would haunt him all his life. Notorious for chain smoking and forgetting to eat when working on an oil deal, Slick occasionally recognized that he was ruining his health:

"I am going to get well no matter how long it takes or how much I lose. It always makes me sad when I think of these things while writing and it hurts me."

— Tom Slick's letter to his mother, 1912

He traveled alone for eight months to some of the most exotic places in the world; to document the adventure, he had his photograph taken in a Chinese rickshaw, one of the few times he posed for a camera. His worries that the trip might have a negative impact on his business were unfounded. In fact, while he was away, Prairie Oil and Gas bought some of his oil leases for one million dollars, an unbelievable sum in those days. Other leases had been developed by his brother, Jesse, and were producing large amounts of oil. When he returned to Oklahoma, he re-entered the oil business with new gusto; and he accepted his friend and former partner Bernard B. Jones's matchmaking offer with equal enthusiasm.

A man who always trusted first impressions, Slick proposed to Berenice Frates soon after they met; and the couple planned an elaborate October wedding. Instead, the ceremony took place just one month later in the Frates' home in Springfield, Missouri, on June 21, 1915, at ten o'clock at night. It was attended only by family and the couple left immediately after their vows, in a private railroad car bound for Clarion, Pennsylvania. It was an unusual beginning, but indicative of the far from ordinary life that they would build together.

While mysterious in the newspaper accounts of the day, the wedding's "shotgun" appearance was explained by the fact that Slick's older brother was seriously ill. It would not have been proper for Berenice – a single woman – to accompany her fiancé to Clarion in 1915. So they married immediately and rushed to Pennsylvania that very night. Jesse recovered, but his health continued to decline; and he died four years later, sending Tom Slick into another of his many depressions over the next decade.

But on May 6, 1916, Slick was far from depressed. In Oklahoma, a new gusher came in, providing him with a now-familiar rush of success. Oil production in the Cushing Field had peaked at 305,000 barrels a day, with most of it sent to fuel U.S. forces fighting in World War I. But the birth of a baby son in Pennsylvania produced a completely new experience. For the rest of his life, Slick would feel the pull between work and family, the joys of homelife competing with his gypsy spirit; and Clarion would remain the place where both feelings co-existed in temporary harmony.

Berenice Frates Slick never much liked the Clarion house; and she ruefully remembered arriving in her husband's hometown on their wedding night, where he presented her with a special gift – "a three story monstrosity" Victorian house across the street from her mother-in-law's home, already completely furnished for the new bride. According to family stories, it took some getting used to. She wrote home with some dismay that the house was terrible, and to make matters worse, "they put sugar in their cornbread up here."

Thomas Bernard Slick was born during that first summer in Clarion, named for his father, with his middle name chosen in honor of the man who introduced his parents. (Later, after a falling out with Bernard Jones, the Slicks would change their son's name to Thomas Baker Slick, Jr.) The next year, their daughter, Betty, was born, followed by Earl in 1923. All three children resembled their father, fair-haired and blue eyed, and somewhat slight in stature.

Slick, Sr., would slip in and out of the scene, moving between Pennsylvania, Oklahoma, Mississippi, Kansas, Texas, and wherever else a deal might beckon. When he was with his family, he captivated them with his unique combination of tenderness and adventuresome spirit. When his little daughter, Betty, had nightmares, he sat by her bed and listened, soothing her back to sleep. They had long conversations about the ghost that Betty heard bumping around the music room on the third floor, deciding it was "friendly." He and young Tom read about the mysterious *"L'Homme des Nieges"* (Snowman) who according to French explorers inhabited a place described as the "Roof of the World", a place the boy decided he'd visit someday; and in early 1923, when Tom was six years old, newspaper stories of the discovery of King Tutankhamen's sarcophagus in Egypt captured his imagination.

Slick's children adored him, accepting the fact that he was a complicated man. Their mother was more remote; and despite her day-to-day presence in their lives, the relationship was rather formal. Decades later, Betty Slick Moorman, now a mother and grandmother herself, would explain, "she was scary," hinting that her father's constant travels were partially to escape Berenice's critical personality.

But summers were special family times in Clarion; and during one of his sojourns there, Slick, Sr. took young Tom to explore the nearby woods. They discovered a fallen log across the river that would eventually become a favorite hideout for Tom and Betty on Sundays, when they played hooky from church and invented all sorts of games and adventures in a natural playground of trees and twisted trails.

But the first time that father and son visited the log, Tom was only five or six years old; and he was frightened when his father urged him to cross the river by walking on the log. The older Sick recognized an opportunity to convey one of his famous "lessons in life."

"A coward dies a thousand deaths; a brave man only one," Slick quoted to his son in their spectacular forest classroom. The little boy seemed to grasp the lesson's meaning; he walked the log. Later in life, he met adult challenges the same way, often remembering his father's words in the Pennsylvania woods and quoting them whenever he crossed new territory where no one else had dared to go.

The woods weren't the only exciting places to visit. Grandmother Mary Slick's house was "huge and haunted, with a hidden tunnel to China in the backyard," according to Betty Slick Moorman, who played there with her older brother. Two maiden aunts named Frances and Margaret lived in another house in the compound; and they provided even more mystery.

"Aunt Frances never spoke a word to us. She was very, very shy; and she never spoke to anyone except her two sisters – my grandmother (Mary Slick) and my Aunt Margaret. But she was so tender and sweet. She would play dolls with me, but she wouldn't speak. She would take Tom and me into her lap and then say to Aunt Margaret, 'Do you think the children would like to stay for dinner?'"

Eccentric Aunt Frances, and her sisters Margaret and Mary, were first generation Pennsylvanians. Their father, Thomas Baker, came to the United States from England in 1843 or 1844, settling with his wife in Shippenville, just five miles west of Clarion. The couple established the first commercial flourmill in town; they prospered and raised eight children in their large home in the center of town.

Mary Baker was the youngest daughter, and during her teens, she met an adventuresome young man named Johnson Slick, whose genealogy is a little sketchier than Mary's. The son of a tailor from Clarion, he left home at fourteen to work in the Bakers' flourmill, where he met Mary. Ten years later, in 1880, they married; and they had three children – Jesse (1880), Tom (1883) and Flored (1888). By 1892, Johnson and Mary Slick were living in Clarion, operating their own flourmill. But when the first oil in the United States was discovered in western Pennsylvania, Slick decided to enter this brand new business as a contract driller. His son, who joined him in the oilfields when he was sixteen years old, would become the largest independent oil operator in the world.

This family history, and the colorful characters who inhabited it, supplied fascinating subjects for discussion as young Tom and Betty Slick sat on the banks of the Clarion River, playing hooky from Sunday school, while their mother took care of baby Earl at home. Stories about how their great-grandparents met behind a flour sack, the secret reason for their shy aunt Frances's silence, why their other grandmother "Muddy" (Lula Montez Buck Frates) whistled before she fainted, had all sorts of plots and sub-plots with mysterious aspects to explore. And eight-year-old Betty, still convinced that at least one of her long-dead ancestors made ghostly visits to the Slick family, playing the piano in the music room, romping in the children's playroom on the third floor, enjoying all the secret nooks of the huge old house that might have been haunted, extracted a promise from her brother to investigate. More than thirty years later he kept that promise.

It's clear from family stories that the King of the Wildcatters encouraged his children's sense of adventure and love of wild landscapes. "Whenever our father came to Clarion to spend time with us in the summer, we always walked down to the river and the woods. He was so busy that he wasn't there much; but when he was, we had wonderful adventures," Betty Slick Moorman recalled more than seventy years later.

Slick never learned to balance work and leisure, although sometimes he made dramatic efforts to do so, recognizing that he had jeopardized his physical and emotional health by his frenetic work pace and lifestyle. His son would not make this same mistake; instead, he integrated work and leisure until they were one and the same.

But like his father, he was a searcher with a gypsy spirit; and both men paid a price for their frequent absences from home. Wives and children never quite understood.

Slick Sr.'s absences took him to Indian Territory in 1907, before he drilled his first big well in Oklahoma, when he was known as "Dry Hole Tom." Years later, now "Lucky Tom" continued the friendships he'd made in the Territory, always treating his Native American partners with a respect and fairness that were rare in those days. From "Dry Hole Tom" to "Lucky Tom", Slick always discounted the importance of luck in the process of oil discovery; however he did give some credit to intuition, experience and knowledge.

"I know all of this country, every foot of it. As a leaser I drove and walked over all of it, studied, have learned to sort of sense, by intuition, where there ought to be oil," he explained when reporters asked how he'd become the world's largest independent oil operator in 1930, with net assets of $17 million.

In more homespun terms, he compared his so-called luck to a flock of ducks. "Did you ever shoot ducks?" he asked the newspapermen. "Lay hidden in a blind and call to the ducks as they fly over, and bring them within range? Same way with Luck. A whole lot of lucky chances may fly past unless you know how to call them, have a good gun, all loaded, and are able to shoot straight."

Not wanting miss any of the lucky chances flying over, Slick Sr. worked ferociously during the 1920s, branching out from his legendary oil successes to partner with his father-in-law, investing in plantations in Mississippi, building railroads, and establishing new townsites in Oklahoma named Slick and Nuyaka. And young Tom watched, and learned, and waited for his turn.

Like all games of chance, the stakes got higher as Slick's businesses expanded; and eventually, his workaholic ways upped the ante to include his physical and mental health. Clarion called him home; and quiet days with family were precious. Throughout the 1920s, as his children Tom, Betty and Earl explored the river and pretended that their woods were mythical kingdoms, Slick Sr. moved between the serenity of his birthplace and the much wilder world beyond. With new advances in technology and transportation, the world was expanding. In 1926, National Broadcasting Company (NBC) linked twenty-four radio stations into the first "network," bringing together news and features from across the United States; and the next year, aviator Charles Lindberg made his historic solo flight across the Atlantic Ocean, flying from New York to Paris in thirty-three and a half hours.

After nearly twenty years in the oil business, Slick was once again exhausted and his family began to plead with him to take a vacation. In March, 1929 he sold all of his oil producing lands to the Prairie Oil & Gas Company for $40 million, announcing that he was going to "rest for a while." Newspaper and magazine articles described the details of the sale, estimating the sold oil fields were yielding about thirty-four thousand barrels a day at the time.

Slick kept part of the royalties on the production he sold to Prairie; and he still had 525,000 acres of leased undeveloped land. One observer remarked that the Slick deal was "like selling the milk but keeping the cows"; and friends and competitors wagered that he would not be able to resist returning to the oil business.

But Slick had promised his family a vacation; and with the huge cash transaction completed, he gave farewell bonuses of $2 million each to his colleagues, E.E. Kirkpatrick of Tulsa, who ran the Slick Company's oil operations, and to Charles Urschel, who was married to his sister, Flored, and had been a business associate for the past ten years.

Slick's health had been poor for several months, but extraction of an infected tooth seemed to have improved it. The family made plans to travel to their second home in San Antonio, Texas, so that Slick could go on to the Gulf Coast to fish, and to his ranch in south Texas to hunt. Just the year before, he had hosted a large group of oilmen at a special dinner at the Tulsa Country Club, where he served nothing but wild game he had killed on his ranch. It was described in the local newspaper as "one of the most successful affairs ever staged on the mid-continent"; and Slick planned to repeat it in the fall with a new supply of wild game.

As the family prepared to travel to Texas, Slick told friends, "I am a mass of nerves and a bundle of nerve. I need a good rest, maybe for a year or so."

Just one month later he was back. In April he filed papers in New York City to incorporate the Tom Slick Oil Company in Oklahoma. Executives of the new company were a familiar cast of characters: Slick was president; his brother-in-law Charles Urschel, was first vice president; E.E. Kirkpatrick was second vice president; and J.H. Grand was Secretary.

The new company began operating out of Tulsa, with an office and activities in Texas as well. The pace was soon intense; and Slick was again in the oil game and back to his workaholic ways.

About a year later, he checked into Johns Hopkins Hospital in

Baltimore after a breakdown, much like the one he had in 1915. He was diagnosed with thyroid disease; and he was so run down that a "rest cure" was prescribed on June 27, 1930, until he was strong enough for surgery to remove a goiter.

On August 5, the operation was performed and surgeons thought it had been successful. As he recovered, the Slick family began to plan a two-week vacation in Canada. Fourteen year old Tom was looking forward to fishing with his father, and to seeing his grandmother, who would travel from Clarion to join them.

But the following Friday Slick had a stroke while sitting on the porch at the hospital. It was followed by a second one, and a cerebral hemorrhage. The King of the Wildcatters was dead at 46.

A special train took his body to his hometown of Clarion for burial; and family, friends, and fellow oilmen from the southwest traveled east to pay tribute to him. Wires and cables of condolence arrived from all parts of the world, indications of the respect and high esteem felt for the oilman, not only by leaders in the industry but also by the men in the field. At 3:30 p.m. on Saturday, as last rites were performed in Clarion, oil wells in Oklahoma and Texas stopped drilling for the rest of the day in honor of the famous wildcatter.

The oil industry had lost a leader; fourteen-year-old Tom had lost a father. As the new decade began, he felt the huge void created by his father's death. He offered comfort to his little sister and brother; and he felt the responsibility of the Tom Slick legacy. He remembered that his father had forged that legacy in the oil fields, claiming that he was "born among the oil derricks. The first sniff of air I ever breathed into my nostrils was laden with the odor of oil."

That odor would permeate the lives of the Slicks for generations – first luring a father to remote oilrigs far from home, later attracting a kidnapper with its scent in the 1930s, and eventually providing the incredible wealth that would open doors to all sorts of strange new worlds for young Tom Slick.

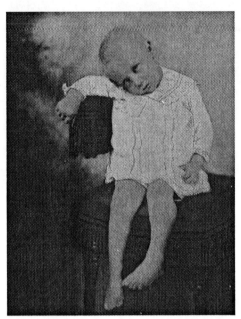

Thomas Baker Slick, Sr. was born in 1883 in Clarion, Pennsylvania. (*Betty Slick Moorman Photo Collection.*)

Berenice Frates was born in 1890, the oldest child of Joseph and Lula Frates. (*Betty Slick Moorman Photo Collection.*)

Joseph Frates was a railroad tycoon and partner of Tom Slick, Sr. His daughter, Berenice, married the "Kind of the Wildcatters" in 1915. (*Betty Slick Moorman Photo Collection.*)

Lula Montez Buck was the most beautiful girl in Leadville, Colorado when Joseph Frates married her in 1889. (*Betty Slick Moorman Photo Collection.*)

After making a huge oil discovery, the Cushing Field in Oklahoma, Tom Slick, Sr,
took a trip around the world to "rest." China, c. 1912. (*Betty Slick Moorman
Photo Collection.*)

Portrait of Berenice Frates prior to her marriage to Tom Slick, Sr.,
in 1915. (*Margaret Urschel Photo Collection.*)

Thomas Baker Slick, Sr., c. 1915. (*Betty Slick Moorman Photo Collection.*)

Tom Slick's wedding present to his bride Berenice was a 3-story Victorian house, completely furnished, in Clarion, Pennsylvania, c. 1915. (*Betty Slick Moorman Photo Collection.*)

Flored Slick, born in 1888, often handled the business end of her older brother's oil business. Her marriage to Charles Urschel further strengthened the relationship. (*Margaret Urschel Photo Collection.*)

Charles Urschel had a business background, and the "King of the Wildcatters" was delighted with his new brother-in-law. (*Margaret Urschel Photo Collection.*)

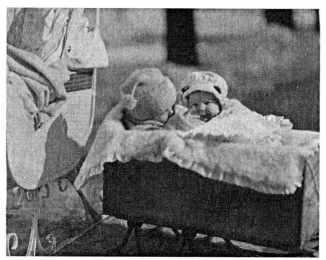

Tom Slick, Jr. and baby sister Betty, 1918. (*Betty Slick Moorman Photo Collection.*)

Betty Slick and baby brother Earl, c.1923. (*Betty Slick Moorman Photo Collection.*)

Flo Slick Urschel with her son Charles, Jr., and her niece and nephews, Betty, Tom, and Earl (in baby carriage) Slick, c 1923. (*Margaret Urschel Photo Collection.*)

Betty and Tom Slick, with first cousin Charles Urschel, Jr., who would become their stepbrother just a few years later, c. 1926. (*Betty Slick Moorman Photo Collection.*)

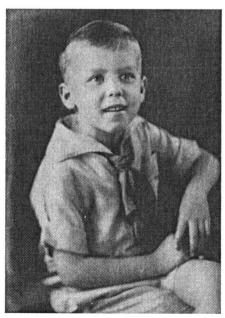

Earl Frates Slick, c. 1928. (*Margaret Urschel Photo Collection.*)

FLOOD EDITION NO. 3

PIONEER OIL HERALD

VOLUME 1, NUMBER 13.   PIONEER, EASTLAND COUNTY, TEXAS, TUESDAY, MAY 19, 1922.   EVERYWHERE 5c

World's Biggest Shallow Oil Field

7500 Barrel Oil Gusher, Slick & Pennant Bryson No. 1 Blew in Roaring Out Bowels of Earth from 2457 ft. Sat. Night

Huge oil discoveries earned Tom Slick Sr. the nickname "King of the Wildcatters,"
c. 1922. (*Betty Slick Moorman Photo Collection.*)

PATRONS ARE REQUESTED TO FAVOR THE COMPANY BY CRITICISM AND SUGGESTION CONCERNING ITS SERVICE

WESTERN UNION

CLASS OF SERVICE		SIGNS
This is a full-rate Telegram or Cablegram unless its deferred character is indicated by a suitable sign above or preceding the address.		DL = Day Letter
		NM = Night Message
		NL = Night Letter
		LCO = Deferred Cable
		NLT = Cable Letter
		WLT = Week-End Letter

NEWCOMB CARLTON, PRESIDENT   J. C. WILLEVER, FIRST VICE-PRESIDENT

The filing time as shown in the date line on full-rate telegrams and day letters, and the time of receipt at destination as shown on all messages, is STANDARD TIME.

Received at

  9G R 26 DL

      OKLAHOMACITY OKLA 511P AUG 18 1930

    C F URSCHEL

          CARE T B SLICK HOME CLARION PENN

    EVERY OPERATION IN OKLAHOMACITY FIELD SHUT DOWN FOR TWO HOURS

    TODAY IN HONOR OF TOM UNION TRANSPORTATION AND OTHER LINES

    SUSPENDED OPERATION AT TULSA DURING FUNERAL

                              E E KIRKPATRICK

                                  839A AUG 19

When Tom Slick, Sr., died in 1930, Oklahoma oil rigs shut down in his honor.

Wife and Three Children Given $75,000,000 Estate

★ ★ ★ ★ ★ ★ ★

Income For Youngsters

Their Share Will Be Made Available in Three Instalments, Paid at Ages of 30, 45 and 55 Years.

CLARION, Pa., Aug. 27.—(P)— An estate estimated at between $75,000,000 and $100,000,000 was disposed of in the will of Thomas B. Slick, independent oil operator, which was probated Wednesday. Slick was reputed to be the wealthiest independent oil operator in the world.

The vast fortune was left to the widow, three children and Slick's mother. While no estimate of the value of the estate was contained in the will, Slick's attorney and others who were closely associated with him provided an estimate of its worth.

The oil operator's mother, Mrs. Mary Slick of Clarion, was provided with $5,000 a year as long as she lives.

The widow, Bernice Slick of Oklahoma City, Okla., was left one third of the remainder of the estate and the remaining two thirds was left in trust to the three children.

The Slick home in Oklahoma City also was left to the widow.

The three children are Thomas B. jr, Betty and Earl. At the age of 18 the daughter will receive $5,000 a year until she is 30 years old. The sons, at the age of 21, will receive $10,000 a year each until they are 30. At the age of 30, each child will get one third of the amount due him or her; at the age of 45 another one third; and the last one third at the age of 55.

The widow, Charles F. Urschel and Arthur A. Seeligson, were appointed trustees and empowered to either sell or carry on the Slick oil operations and other business.

The will was drawn in Baltimore, Md., on July 15, 1930; while Slick a patient at Johns Hopkins hospital. Slick died at the hospital and the body was buried here, his boyhood home.

The oil operator was known as "the king of the wildcatters." He engaged in operations throughout the southwest.

Slick State Tax May Total $9,500,000

Mrs.
Tom
Slick
Becomes
Oil
Operator
Under
Terms
Of
"Wildcat
King's"
Will

Mrs. Tom B. Slick

By the will of her late husband filed in Clarion, Pa., Wednesday, Mrs. Thomas B. Slick becomes one of Oklahoma's most important oil operators. One-third of the huge estate becomes her's, and in addition she is named one of the three trustees who will administer the holdings of the "king of the wildcatters." No ... in the actual machinery of operation of the Slick ...

Executors for Tom Slick Sr.'s estate were his brothers-in-law, Charles Urschel (married to his sister Flored) and Arthur Seeligson (married to Berenice's sister Ramona). The estate was tremendous for 1930; and publicity surrounded it for months. (*Partial article, courtesy of the* Daily Oklahoman.)

41

Chapter Three

Alone
(The 1930s)

Oklahoma City was booming in the 1930s, and oil was the impetus. The Slick mansion on Eighteenth Street was a beautiful three-story Victorian, with a large wooden porch that circled the house. Moving between their houses in Pennsylvania and Oklahoma had become a way of life for the family, but now that she was widowed, Berenice Slick moved south, joining her parents and several siblings. The summer of 1930 was a sad one; and Tom and Betty particularly missed their father.

In a gesture of family support that was more common in those days, Berenice's youngest sister, Ramona, her husband Arthur Seeligson, and their two sons, Arthur and Frates, moved in with the Slicks. Seeligson was an attorney, and the executor of his brother-in-law's huge estate. He was also a kind, family-oriented man who provided fatherly support to the young Slick children. Tom, Betty and Earl were delighted to have their cousins living in the house; and their activities and laughter eased a very difficult time.

In 1931 the family consolidated still more. Charles Urschel, Slick's oil partner and brother-in-law, had become a widower the year before Slick died. His deceased wife, Flored, and Tom Slick, Sr., were sister and brother; and the families were close during the early wildcatting days and through their rise to wealth and social status. After a brief courtship, Urschel married Berenice; and his son, Charles, Jr., was now a stepbrother to Tom, Betty and Earl, in addition to being a first cousin.

The death of his father when Tom was 14 years old contributed to the boy's sense of responsibility, which he felt for the rest of his life. Despite his mother's remarriage, and the eventual success and security that his sister and brother would establish, he assumed the role of "the man of the family."

Betty and Earl both described their big brother as a gentle leader, someone they turned to for advice and support; and family and friends that came along later reported the same.

After ninth grade at Classen High School in Oklahoma City, Tom was enrolled at Phillips Exeter Academy, a respected preparatory school in New Hampshire that listed some very impressive alumni, including one U.S. president (Ulysses S. Grant), three governors of New Hampshire, several Secretaries of State, and many well-known scholars, authors, and college presidents. As early as 1908, the school could claim that graduates of Exeter had held all the major offices in Presidential cabinets.

Education in the United States was undergoing real change. While many of the "self-made" men of the early 1900s had made fortunes without much schooling, they wanted more for their own children. Slick, Sr., had not even completed high school when he left home for the oilfields; much more was expected of his son Tom.

But according to his aunt Ramona, his earliest days at Exeter "were no indication of his future achievements." She remembers traveling by train from Oklahoma City to New Hampshire, with her husband, Arthur, sister Berenice, and fourteen-year-old Tom. They stopped briefly in New York City, to see the newly completed Empire State Building, the tallest building in the world.

"Tom was an overweight, reluctant and unhappy teenager," she recalled nearly seventy years later. "And unfortunately, added to this, his face had a purplish ointment look, due to prolonged treatment for impetigo. Only someone who truly loved him would have had the heart and nerve to claim him as family before any Admissions Board, much less Exeter."

The first few weeks were filled with constant requests to come home. He was lonely, and academically he was not prepared for the elite prep school. Everything was wrong with the northeast; and Tom began to think of creative reasons why he need to come home.

A letter to his mother in November explained that everyone at school had a "horrible Eastern disease called 'pink eye'; only returning to Oklahoma would prevent his infection. The Urschels were unyielding; and Tom began to consider his other options, a characteristic for coping with challenges that he would refine and call on throughout his life.

He discovered a beautiful room on the fifth floor of Phillips Hall, with Chinese green walls and rows of dark brown books, circles of comfortable chairs, and a mahogany rostrum for public speaking. He learned that Exeter was famous for the ancient avocation of its young men – public speaking – and debate became a new tool for making friends and "convincing enemies." Squash also captured his enthusiasm; and he became the team captain by his senior year.

Exeter also offered state-of-the-art science laboratories, where Tom experimented in chemistry and physics; and the school's Preventive Medicine Infirmary definitely was ahead of its time, reporting that the use of ultra-violet treatments had built up resistance to the common cold amongst the student body. The teenager was fascinated; and by the time he went home for summer vacation, he was an Exeter man.

In the summer of 1933, the Slick/Urschel family was in Oklahoma City. Shortly after 11:00 p.m. on Saturday, July 22, two men with guns walked onto the front porch of the Urschel mansion, where a friendly bridge game was underway in the cool evening air. Berenice screamed.

"Stop that or we'll blow your heads off," George "Machine Gun" Kelly is reported to have said. He asked which man was Charles Urschel, and when neither replied, Kelly and his accomplice, Albert Bates, loaded both Urschel and his bridge partner, Walter Jarrett, into a waiting automobile.

Once the kidnappers were outside of town, they searched their captives' wallets and quickly discovered which was Urschel. Taking the fifty-one dollars in Jarrett's wallet, they pushed him out of the car onto a country road and drove away.

Meanwhile, the wives had run inside and called the police. Just a few years before, the Lindberg kidnapping had horrified the world; and the women were terrified. The police immediately put Berenice in touch with J. Edgar Hoover, Director of the FBI in Washington,

DC; and within an hour, the house was filled with local police, federal agents, and the press.

Soon, everyone had a good description of the kidnappers from both wives, and from Jarrett, who arrived back at the house around 3:00 a.m., tired and bedraggled. There is some evidence that the kidnappers had originally planned to take fifteen-year-old Betty, based mainly on the fact that the teenager reported seeing the two men following her on two occasions earlier that week.

Urschel and newly elected president Franklin D. Roosevelt were friends; and Hoover recognized that it would be essential to crack the case fast.

While lawmen and federal agents in Oklahoma City began an intense investigation, Kelly arrived at his gang's hideout near Paradise, Texas, a five-hundred-acre ranch that belonged to his wife's stepfather, "Boss Shannon". Urschel was blindfolded and handcuffed and taken to shack adjacent to the ranch house, where he remained captive for nine days. Kelly read him the newspaper headlines about the kidnapping, and informed Urschel that there were too many federal agents working on the case to safely send a ransom demand to his wife in Oklahoma City.

A creative thinker, Urschel suggested using a family friend in Tulsa, John Catlett, as a messenger; and the kidnappers gave him a pencil and paper and instructed him to write two notes – one to Catlett and one to his wife.

As the ransom note made its way towards Oklahoma, Urschel was learning as much about his surroundings as he could; and despite his blindfold, he collected valuable information that would later help the FBI. He noticed that he could hear airplanes fly overhead twice a day; and when they did, he asked his captors what time it was. Later he would tell federal agents that at 9:45 every morning, and at 5:45 in the afternoon, planes flew over the hideout. Since there were far fewer flights in 1933, this clue would be of major assistance in pinpointing the location of the hideout. He also had as many conversations as possible with everyone at the Shannon ranch, learning that Bates did not think much of the famous bank robbing couple Bonnie and Clyde, and carefully remembering a new name Harvey Bailey when he arrived at the ranch with a wounded leg. He left his fingerprints on everything he could touch, hoping they would someday provide evidence that he was there.

On July 26, a messenger delivered a large envelope to the Catlett home in Tulsa. It contained the two notes from Urschel, and a ransom letter from the kidnappers to E.E. Kirkpatrick, an oilman/rancher and newspaperman, who was also a close family friend. It demanded two hundred thousand dollars, and gave instructions for delivering it.

The kidnappers wanted "genuine used federal reserve currency"; and they outlined exactly what the Urschel family should next. Following directions, they ran this ad in the *Daily Oklahoman* newspaper:

FOR SALE – 160 acres land, good five-room house, deep well. Also cows, tools, tractors, corn and hay. $3,750.00
For quick sales TERMS

Two days after the ad ran, an airmail letter arrived at the newspaper, postmarked Joplin, Missouri, instructing Kirkpatrick to board the train for Kansas City on the night of July 29. He was told to travel alone, and to watch for two successive bonfires on the right side of the track. Once he saw the second fire, he was to throw the ransom money off the train. The kidnappers said Urschel would be permitted to return home once they received the money. They also provided a contingency plan in case something went wrong, telling Kirkpatrick to check into the Muehlebach Hotel in Kansas City under the name of E.E. Kincaid and wait for further instructions.

The Urschel family withdrew the money from First National Bank of Oklahoma City; and the FBI recorded all the serial numbers. Catlett boarded the train with Kirkpatrick, which he was not supposed to do. Whether the kidnappers knew this, or as some sources report, Kelly had car trouble and could not set the bonfires in time, Kirkpatrick and Catlett had an uneventful train ride to Kansas City, and they checked into the hotel late Saturday night.

The following morning, a telegram arrived, promising to contact Kirkpatrick later that day. The telephone in Kirkpatrick's room rang at 5:45 p.m. on Sunday, July 30. A man's voice directed him to take a taxi to the LaSalle Hotel and walk west, with the suitcase containing the money in his right hand. This time the instructions were followed almost exactly – Kirkpatrick did tuck a gun in his belt – and Kelly met him on Linwood Boulevard, saying "I'll take that grip," assuring him that Urschel would be home in twelve hours.

Family and friends remember the incredible tension of the entire week, and the excruciating wait on July 31. While Kelly and Bates divided the money at the Shannon ranch, they debated about what to do with Urschel, finally opting not to kill him. After allowing him to bathe and shave, they drove through rain to the outskirts of Oklahoma City, warning him not to talk about his kidnapping. They told him to walk a few miles to a gas station where he could call for help; and they gave him ten dollars for cab fare. Around nine o'clock that night, Charles Urschel arrived at his home. Berenice and the children were waiting, along with the FBI. The manhunt for the kidnappers would begin the next day.

With the information that Urschel supplied about airplanes flying over at specific times, the FBI was able to pinpoint the Shannon ranch; and on August 12, a raiding party of federal agents, local police, and Urschel arrived. Harvey Bailey was there, with several others who had just robbed the Peoples National Bank in Kingfisher, Oklahoma. The gang was arrested, along with Boss Shannon, his wife Ora, and son and daughter-in-law. Some of the ransom money and machine guns belonging to Kelly were collected as evidence.

That same day, Bates was arrested in Denver, Colorado, when he tried to use stolen money orders from an earlier bank robbery. George and Kathryn Kelly were on the run, growing more nervous as they learned of each new arrest.

Amidst the summer drama, Tom was packing for his senior year at Exeter. Before leaving for New Hampshire, he saw an odd-looking envelope arrive at home, with a note threatening the entire Urschel/Slick family if the Shannons were convicted. The chase for the Kellys intensified, taking some bizarre twists; and on September 26, just as Tom was getting settled at school, the gangsters were arrested in Memphis. They were extradited to Oklahoma and tried for kidnapping Charles Urschel.

The trial was well documented since it set many new legal precedents for kidnapping cases. It was dramatic and colorful; and the jury deliberated for less than an hour before finding George and Kathryn Kelly guilty on October 12, 1933. They were sentenced to life in prison; and Kathryn Kelly would say on many future occasions that she wished they had killed Charles Urschel.

The Urschels, and members of their extended family that included siblings, aunts, uncles, and cousins, never forgot the terror of the kidnapping. As young Tom, Betty, Earl and stepbrother Charles grew up, they avoided publicity and worried for several generations that somehow the Kellys and their gang would seek retribution.

Years later, Urschel visited Kelly in prison and reported that he was "a changed man". The kidnapper died in prison in 1954, one day after his fifty-fourth birthday. Kathryn Kelly was paroled in 1958, after twenty-five years in prison, and died in Tulsa, Oklahoma, at the age of eighty-one.

But as Tom prepared to graduate from Exeter in the spring of 1934, the Kellys were in prison and no longer a threat to his family. He saw an exciting future taking shape, starting with a wonderful graduation present from his grandfather, Joseph Frates.

Frates held a special place in Tom's heart. The boy resonated with his adventuresome spirit; and his love of hunting, fishing and traveling reminded him of the father he missed. When the school term ended in 1934, Tom and Betty Slick, and their stepbrother Charles Urschel, all completed the year with honors. Berenice wanted to show her appreciation and asked her children what they would like. Tom suggested a trip to some foreign country, accompanied by his grandfather. Charles was quick to sign on to the idea.

"I was delighted, and the trip was planned," Frates wrote in his diary. "Betty, of course, was included in the award; but she wanted something else." Charles was attending Culver Military Academy in Indiana; Tom was at Phillips Exeter Academy in New Hampshire; and Betty was at the Miss Madeira School in Virginia. The extended family attended the end of term at all the schools, and completed the circuit at Exeter Academy on June 23, 1934.

On June 30, Joseph Frates boarded the *S.S. Monarch of Bermuda* from the docks of Lower Manhattan, with his grandsons Tom Slick, Jr., and Charles Urschel, Jr.. The send-off party consisted of Charles and Berenice Urschel, Arthur and Ramona Seeligson, Mrs. Joseph Frates, Betty and Earl Slick, Earl Frates, and two schoolmates of Tom Slick's – Fred Kemple and Kemp Gugglemann. Powerful tugboats pulled the ship out of the harbor, to the shoutings of "bon voyage."

Tom Slick's first ocean voyage, accompanied by his grandfather and stepbrother, was destined for Rio de Janeiro, Brazil. Bermuda, Cuba, Panama, Colombia, Ecuador, Peru, the Guano Islands, Chile, Bolivia, and Argentina were on the itinerary prior to Brazil; and the return journey included traveling over the mouth of the Amazon, past Cayenne and Devils Island, French Guiana, Venezuela, Trinidad, the Virgin Islands, Puerto Rico, Santo Domingo, and Haiti, finally reaching Miami, Florida and returning to Oklahoma City, Oklahoma.

"We traveled by steam railroads, cog railroads, steamships, sea planes, and automobiles," Joseph Frates wrote in an account he circulated to family members as a Christmas present in December, 1934. "We saw a great many interesting places, natives of many different countries and languages, came in contact with some high class people, well informed on conditions throughout the world, visited one country where war was, and still is, in progress with an adjoining nation, another where civil war was in progress. We also passed through the greatest inland waterway in the world – the Panama Canal."

Diaries record Tom's enthusiasm for everything new and exotic; and his grandfather chuckled when he ordered every unusual item on each foreign menu, sometimes "paying for it" the next day.

"While we were on this trip, Tom was continually complaining about the foods; there were too many American dishes; he wanted native foods, something he couldn't get at home," Frates wrote in his diary. In Rio de Janeiro, the travelers were entertained by friends who ran Standard Oil's operations in Brazil. Aware of young Tom's desire to sample native foods, they went to a restaurant that served a local specialty – an octopus dinner.

"When the dish was served, I took a small bite and I want to tell you right now it was terrible," Frates wrote, "but of course I said nothing. Looking around the table I noticed that our hosts were eating sparingly. I am not sure how the fish affected Tom; however I do know that he was looking for pills that evening; and to the best of my knowledge, there was no further complaint from Tom about American food during the rest of the tour."

Tom and Charles explored every corner of the elegant ship, befriended the crew, and were sought after by young ladies on the dance floor. During the last days in Rio, Tom bought a monkey as a present for his younger brother Earl. Nicknamed "Johnny," the pet was mischievous, and, according to Frates, "One evening Johnny got loose, and what he did to things in Charles' and Tom's rooms was plenty; the rooms looked like a cyclone had struck them."

The travelers departed the elegant Hotel Gloria, Oklahoma bound, with Johnny in tow. A twin-engine, twenty-two-passenger seaplane operated by Pan American Airlines flew them to Miami; and they completed their journey by train.

When Tom returned to Oklahoma to pack for his freshman year at Yale University in New Haven, Connecticut, he had no doubt that he would travel to every corner of the world in the years ahead.

Slick was a member of Pierson College at Yale; and he lived alone at 74 Wall Street. By the end of the year, he was second in his class, pursuing a pre-medical course of study. He entered athletics with enthusiasm, with great success on the squash and crew teams; and his love of public speaking, acquired at Exeter, eventually earned him a "high oration appointment" during his junior year.

Albert Einstein said that imagination was more important than knowledge; but Slick believed both were essential. His outstanding record at Yale, culminating in Phi Beta Kappa, reflects his love of knowledge; and his sister Betty reported that "he had enough imagination for everyone."

Only a year apart in school, they often spent college weekends together. Betty was attending Vassar College nearby; and she introduced her handsome brother to several attractive girls. She was already in love with Lew Moorman, whom she would marry in 1940; and wonderful memories of double-dating still were vibrant many decades later.

According to Betty, Tom's pursuits in college – both scientific and romantic – were legendary. "His interest at the time was in the possibility of cross breeding various and sundry animal types and species. He carried in his wallet a list of possibilities, such as camel and horse, cow and buffalo – which was actually done later, but not by Tom – culminating in ape and man. His girlfriends viewed this list with mixed emotions and did not always find it amusing.

"The only concrete accomplishment to result from this interest was his purchase of the 'Hoat', more affectionately known as Sweet William. Tom had read in *Ripley's Believe It Or Not* about a farmer who had raised an animal that was presumably a cross between a hog and a goat. He sought out the farmer and purchased the 'Hoat', which he kept at our mother's farm near Oklahoma City.

"Sweet William was a disreputable looking, deformed creature – high in the front, low in the back, with scraggly goat hair and an equally scraggly hog's tail. The goat tendency to be a horned animal centered in his hooves, which grew outward and upward, forming almost a complete circle. It was as if he walked on rockers.

"Tom exposed Sweet William to both goats and hogs for breeding purposes, but nothing happened. He probably was sexless, or so unattractive that no self-respecting goat or hog would have anything to do with him. Sweet William died a natural but early death. Luckily for all of us, Tom's scientific interests began to find expression in other ways."

Interest in the Loch Ness Monster inspired Slick to organize a trip to Scotland with several fraternity brothers during the summer of 1937. The young men explored the local pubs, played golf on the famous course at St. Andrews, but did not see anything of interest emerge from the famous lake. Slick later told his mother that he had proven something important on his expedition, "that science and fun can co-exist."

By his senior year at Yale, he was seriously dating Betty Lewis, a Vassar classmate of his sister's, from Dallas, Texas. The romance was volatile, since both were extremely intelligent and opinionated. "If Tom said something was blue, Betty said it was red," friends would say years later.

The summer of 1938 was a happy one for the Slick/Urschel family. Tom graduated from Yale, Phi Beta Kappa; and Betty Slick was sure that her handsome beau, Lew Moorman, was the man of her dreams. Later that fall, their younger cousin Arthur Seeligson, Jr., followed a new family tradition and enrolled at Yale.

Tom accompanied young Arthur to New Haven, and sixty-two years later Seeligson remembered it as a very special time. "Tom was like a big brother to me; and it meant so much to have him there. And we shared a very unexpected adventure that fall, one I'll never forget."

The "adventure" was the famous Great Hurricane of New England, one of the most powerful and destructive storms ever to strike the East Coast. The hurricane made a twelve-day journey across the Atlantic and up the eastern seaboard before crashing ashore in Long Island on September 21. The eye was in New Haven, and so were the two cousins.

Winds of more than 120 miles an hour, and storm tides reaching eighteen feet ripped across Connecticut. Downtown Providence, Rhode Island, was submerged under twenty feet of water. New England was devastated. More than fifteen thousand homes were damaged, and 8,900 were totally destroyed. More than six thousand boats were either destroyed or badly damaged; 564 people died, and more than 1,700 were injured. Downed power lines touched off fires across Connecticut; and flooding washed away roadways and sections of the New York, New Haven, and Hartford railroad lines.

Seeligson remembered how glad he was that his older cousin was with him, how they listened together to the howling winds and talked about the incredible power of nature. Slick believed that storms, earthquakes, erupting volcanoes, and other natural forces were humbling experiences, reminders of a much larger universe where man was but "a tiny speck." He was certain that scientific research would help to harness some of these energy sources and mysteries to improve human life; but he also was convinced that some phenomena would remain unexplained. He was comfortable with the dichotomy; he liked a world where logic, imagination, and mystery interacted in a special dance.

He brought the same forces to romantic life; and when he learned that his college sweetheart, Betty Lewis, was thinking of marrying his rival, John Young, Slick used his charm and proven oration skills to convince her not to. Energized by the challenge of competition, he sent flowers and thoughtful notes; and in January, 1939, she accepted his proposal of marriage.

Betty came from a prominent Texas family, and had been presented as a debutante in Dallas during the previous season. But with a degree in child psychology from Vassar, she intended to establish a career. Her father, William Lewis, sensed that his intelligent, strong-minded daughter was not going to be happy with the equally intelligent, strong-minded Slick. But the young couple was determined, and their April wedding in Dallas was described in all the social columns as a splendid event.

But the marriage was volatile; and when Betty was pregnant with their first child, she moved from Oklahoma City back to Dallas, near her parents. The couple separated before the baby was born in August, 1943; they divorced in 1944. William Lewis Slick was named for his grandfather. His parents agreed to set aside their own bitter feelings about the short-lived marriage; and while not always successful, they tried to create a normal childhood for their son. Within a year Betty married John Young; and Slick experienced feelings of loss. But true to his nature, traits he had developed in childhood soon persevered. He did not fret for long. Instead, he accepted "outcome," as he would during all of his less than successful experiences; and he focused on the future. A new decade was beginning; a world war would soon overshadow all else.

When his father died in 1930, Tom Slick was fourteen years old. He assumed the role of the man of the family; and his feelings of responsibility for others would last all his life. (*Margaret Urschel Photo Collection.*)

Widow Berenice Slick married her brother-in-law, widower Charles Urschel, in 1932. Charles, Jr. was both a first cousin and a stepbrother to young Tom, Betty and Earl Slick. (*Margaret Urschel Photo Collection.*)

Family vacation with cousins in Santa Monica, California, c. 1934. Left to right, Berenice Urschel, Charles Urschel, Jr., Arthur Seeligson, Jr., Frates Seeligson, Betty Slick, Tom Slick, Jr. (*Betty Slick Moorman Photo Collection.*)

During the summer of 1934, Joseph Frates took his grandsons Tom Slick and Charles Urschel, Jr., on a lengthy adventure trip to South America. The journey began on an elegant steamship named the S.S. Bermuda. (*Photograph by Joseph Frates.*)

Before reaching South America, the ship stopped in Cuba; where the group enjoyed a tour of Havana. (*Photograph by Joseph Frates.*)

George "Machine Gun" Kelly is arrested in Memphis, Tennessee, for the kidnapping of Charles Urschel, Sr., on September 26, 1933.

Charles Urschel, Sr. (center) and brother-in-law Arthur Seeligson (right), at the trial of "Machine Gun" Kelly, October 1933.

Famous FBI-man Gus Jones captured Machine Gun Kelly, who is reported to have screamed, "Don't shoot G-Man!" Jones remained a lifelong friend of Charles Urschel. (*Margaret Urschel Photo Collection.*)

Goose hunts in south Texas were a favorite sport. From left, James Ellis, Tom Slick, Buell Wright, Charles Urschel, Jr., and Chester Emil. (*Margaret Urschel Photo Collection.*)

Betty Slick, c. 1938. (*Betty Slick Moorman Photo Collection.*)

Like his brothers Tom and Earl Slick, Charles Urschel, Jr., was interested in aviation. (*Margaret Urschel Photo Collection.*)

In addition to Betty Slick, and Betty Young, still another Betty would join the family – beautiful Betty Hailes from California, engaged to Charles Urschel, Jr. (*Margaret Urschel Photo Collection.*)

Tom and Earl Slick, groom and Best Man, 1939. (*Betty Slick Moorman Photo Collection.*)

At the bachelor party for Tom Slick's wedding to Betty Lewis, Slick dressed formally and his groomsmen came as cowboys. (*Betty Slick Moorman Photo Collection.*)

Betty Lewis was both glamorous and intelligent, with a degree from Vassar College. (*Wedding Engagement Announcement photo courtesy of* The Dallas Morning News.)

The groom was equally dashing and brilliant, with a degree from Yale University. (*Betty Slick Moorman Photo Collection.*)

Charles Urschel, Jr., married Betty Heil in the church at Stanford University, where she had graduated with honors. (*Margaret Urschel Photo Collection.*)

Chapter Four

Dreaming Big
The 1940s

In June, 1940, German planes bombed Paris, and five years later the first atomic bomb was dropped by the Americans on Hiroshima, Japan, killing more than fifty thousand people and bringing an end to World War II. Post-war inventions like the long-playing record in 1948 and instant cake-mix in 1949 seemed to promote a sense of well-being in the United States, as half a world away, the Communist People's Republic of China was proclaimed. Tom Slick was a young man in his twenties, patriotic about his country, fascinated by science, and already thinking about ways he might use his family wealth to make the world a better place.

During the 1930s and 1940s, many large oil family dynasties, including the Slick/Urschel family, moved their home bases from Oklahoma to Texas. The reason was twofold: many of their major wells were located there, and there was no state income tax. In 1939, Tom and Earl Slick established the Slick-Urschel Oil Company in partnership with their stepfather and stepbrother, Charles Urschel Sr. and Jr. in San Antonio.

About this time, the senior Urschels built a spectacular home in the city's most exclusive suburb, designed by one of the leading architects of the times, John Staub. Berenice's youngest sister Ramona and her husband Arthur Seeligson joined the migration to San Antonio and built another beautiful mansion just a block away.

In March, 1940, Betty Slick married her beloved Lew Moorman; and the social columns described every detail of the stylish event, including her spectacular wedding cake, which had arrived by train. On June 18, 1940, twenty-four-year-old Tom Slick bought a sixteen-hundred-acre tract of land on the outskirts of his new hometown;

and during the next twelve months, he acquired more land in the area, including the five-thousand-acre Cable Ranch, to bring his long time dream of establishing a "Science City" on the Texas prairie to reality. He named his new ranch ESSAR, chosen to reflect his interest in scientific research, an acronym of sorts, combining an "s" for science and an "r" for research, and spelled ESSAR. Slick's plan for the site was that it would become a center for basic and applied research organizations to cluster, where information would be shared and discoveries made that could improve the world.

At the close of 1941, just one week after Pearl Harbor was bombed by the Japanese, Slick established the first of five scientific research institutes that he would found before he was forty years old. The Foundation of Applied Research (later becoming the Southwest Foundation for Research and Education, and finally, Southwest Foundation for Biomedical Research) was located at ESSAR Ranch; the dream was moving forward. He endowed it with an oilfield. Tom Slick was twenty-five years old.

"Science gives us a tool of unparalleled effectiveness by which we can improve the physical side of our lives; and since science recognizes no boundaries, the lives of people all over the world," he told his family as he arranged for oil royalties to insure the new institute's future.

Slick had developed a list of criteria for all of his diverse projects, one that would evolve into a formula for life. He followed it each time he founded a new non-profit organization; when he developed innovations in agriculture, cattle breeding, oil exploration, and construction; and when he organized expeditions to the Himalayas in search of unexplained phenomena.

He started with a mystery, an unanswered question, a point of wonder. He assembled a team of experts. He planned a "capture" (of information, new oil wells, or yetis for example). He insisted on a thorough investigation held to rigorous standards. And finally, results were shared whatever the outcome of the endeavor.

"I don't believe in failure," Slick said often, "only outcome."

"When there is a disappointment of some sort, I never think it is the end of the story. I believe it's the beginning of something new, sometimes a great adventure." Whether a scientific experiment, a new business venture, or a promising personal relationship, Slick's endeavors were imbued with optimism. And whatever the result, he found new opportunity.

With the outbreak of war in the Pacific, Slick volunteered for naval duty, but poor eyesight disqualified him. Determined to do his duty, he found another opportunity. In 1941 he joined the War Production Board in Washington, DC, and was sent to Chile, attached to the American Embassy in Santiago. His years in the military are not well documented; and many official records have disappeared. There have always been rumors within the family that he was involved in special intelligence projects; but no real evidence has been found; and the CIA has no record of any work Slick may have done for its predecessor, the OSS (Office of Strategic Services).

Slick traveled often during the early 1940s, a bit mysteriously; and when the Navy relaxed its eyesight standards in 1943, he was commissioned as an Ensign for two years, taking courses at Harvard Business School and MIT in the summer of 1944 as a Government War Student. He was assigned to bases in Hawaii (as a liaison officer with the Oahu Railroad), Saipan (as commanding officer of an oil tank farm), and finally to occupied Japan.

When Slick returned to San Antonio from his war duty, he met beautiful 18-year-old Polly Nixon, the daughter of a prominent Texas medical family (also originally from Pennsylvania) that was part of his mother's and stepfather's circle of friends. Nearing thirty, Slick was attracted to her youthful enthusiasm and femininity; and she seemed determined to become the perfect wife.

But the Nixons had reservations. Slick was divorced, something that was less accepted in the 1940s, and he was twelve years older than their daughter. They faced a difficult dilemma, caught between their friendship with the Urschel family and their dreams that their daughter would attend college and eventually marry a man closer to her own age.

The young couple was not deterred; the potential of it all was irresistible. While Slick saw a beautiful young woman willing to be molded into an ideal wife; Polly saw a handsome, worldly man who could provide her with everything she wanted, the fairytale prince that all girls dream might come their way. So despite some resistance from their parents, they became engaged and planned their own wedding in New York.

Family members from both sides traveled by train to New York; and the Pierre Hotel provided a sophisticated, elegant setting for the wedding entourage. Slick's stepbrother, Charles Urschel, Jr., was Best Man; and the bride's twin sister, Patty Nixon, was Maid of Honor..

Riverside Church in Manhattan was not far from the Pierre, and the wedding party began to assemble for a stylish six o'clock ceremony on September 4, 1946. But when the bride's older brother, Jim Nixon, did not arrive at the appointed hour; tension mounted. Nearly sixty years later, Nixon remembers his late arrival, the realization that his watch had stopped, and everyone's relief when the organ music began. Dr. Nixon walked his petite, dark-haired daughter down the aisle; her huge dark eyes, creamy complexion, and elaborate ivory lace veil were a lovely vision; and everyone hoped the fairytale was real.

After a month-long honeymoon in Europe, the newlyweds returned to Texas, settling at ESSAR Ranch, in the old Cable House, an eighteen-room mansion that had once been the winter home of railroad tycoon P.L. Cable.

Later that same year, Slick met Travis Richardson, a straight-talking wrangler who had worked along the Mexican border in World War II, in intelligence. Fluent in Spanish, his assignment had been to work up and down the Rio Grande River, investigating rumors that the Japanese were planning to invade the United States from Mexico.

After the war, Richardson settled in Laredo, Texas, with his wife, Dorothy – a warm-hearted woman who understood wanderlust and enjoyed it. Tom Slick met the Richardsons in 1946, liked them immediately, and asked them to move to ESSAR Ranch so that Travis could run its farming operation.

Nearly sixty years later, Richardson remembers his answer. "I've always enjoyed cattle more than anything," he told Slick wistfully. "I don't think I would like just farming."

The thirty year old Slick considered the situation, and did what would become a pattern in the years ahead. He liked the man; so he adjusted the job description to fit, agreeing to add cattle to existing farming operations.

Over the next few years, the family business consortium (Tom Slick and younger brother, Earl, brother-in-law Lew Moorman, and stepbrother Charles Urschel, Jr.) bought a total of five ranches in south Texas and Oklahoma. The Richardsons lived on all of them, working with Slick on cattle deals, as promised. But Tom Slick could never just follow the established road; and soon, he and Travis were pushing the frontiers of the industry. By 1948, they developed a new breed – a cross between Brahman cattle from India, heat-tolerant and insect resistant, and the Scottish Angus, known for its superb meat quality.

"Tom was the first to develop the Brangus breed," Richardson said in 2001, sitting in the den of his ranch house in Pandora, Texas, filled with photos of adventures with Slick. "He had been to India and Scotland ... and so many other places too; and he had studied the cattle everywhere he visited. He had the idea that breeding the hearty Brahman with the tastier Angus would produce better beef in cattle that could be heat and insect resistant ... perfect for Texas."

There were some Brahman and Angus cattle at the University of Louisiana; and Slick worked with scientists there to produce "Old Zero," a Brangus bull that eventually was taken to Clear Creek Ranch in Welch, Oklahoma (where the famous "hoat" once lived), and Travis Richardson was in charge of the entire Brangus operation by 1948.

In 1949, the International Brangus Breeders Association was established to oversee the careful registration of the new breed, defined strictly as three-eighths Brahman and five-eighths Angus, solid black, polled as to conformation and breed character.

Because the two "parent breeds" are outstanding in their respective strong traits, the Brangus is considered to be the "best of both," declared the "number one American breed," according to the United States Department of Agriculture.

The Brahman, through rigorous natural selection, developed disease resistance and overall hardiness. These cattle are docile, heat tolerant, and have strong mothering instincts. They have outstanding milk production, even under low feed conditions, and calving ease due to a large birth canal and small birth weight. Brahman cattle are noted for their longevity.

The Angus is considered the premier breed for beef quality, marbling at an earlier age than most breeds and reaching the desired grade and weight sooner. Early puberty, high fertility, and good milking ability contribute to the breed's success in breeding with the hearty Brahman.

"Tom was an amazing man," Richardson said as his wife served a gourmet lunch that included Brangus steaks in remote south Texas. "I would be in his office, and anybody in the world could call him and he would talk to them. His whole thrust was to help his fellow man, no matter what the venture.

"He didn't give a hoot in hell about making money on Brangus. He just hoped the breed would help people in poor, hot countries."

While the cattle at ESSAR, Clear Creek and the other ranches flourished, Polly did not like the remote surroundings; and Slick's constant travels put a strain on the "fairytale" relationship that his young wife had envisioned. In 1947, they moved into town. Their daughter, Patty, was born in 1948, followed by son Tom in 1949, and Charles in 1951.

Slick organized his busy life to include short times spent with his family in San Antonio, always insuring that they were filled with special fun, just as his father had done. But also like his father, long times were spent away from home – pursuing the new ideas that were pouring out of his research institutes, buying new ranchlands and experimenting with agribusiness, exploring new oil deals, and even looking to the sky for new projects.

In 1946, Earl Slick, who had flown in the U.S. Air Force in World War II, suggested to his older brother that they establish an airline devoted to cargo, rather than passengers. Slick Airways was the first airline to use the Douglas DC6A; and for a while it led other carriers in market share. In some ways it was ahead of its time, given the success of Federal Express and other air cargo companies today; and by the mid-fifties TWA and the Flying Tiger Lines were vying to purchase it.

Following World War II, the Army had a surplus of Curtiss C 46 airplanes, which had functioned as the "workhorses" for moving equipment, supplies and troops throughout Europe and the South Pacific. Earl Slick saw the chance for a bargain, and bought nine of them for $247,000, against a cost of around $200,000 each to the Army. An article in the July, 1950 issue of *Fortune Magazine* reported that "Earl Slick was so determined to get into the air-freight business without any idea of what they were going to fly or where."

They flew everything from fresh cut flowers and okra to heavier loads like prize bulls and a six-ton bearing destined for U.S. Steel in Pittsburgh. The organization employed mostly war veterans; and their dedication to the company made Slick Airways unique. Complex struggles with passenger airlines including American, United, and TWA, which saw the freight airline as a potential competitor, and with the Civil Aviation Bureau for certification to operate as a common carrier were costly; and bitter battles over freight rates also affected the company's profits. Tom Slick and Charles Urschel had returned their focus to their oil business after a few years, while Earl Slick and Lew Moorman kept the dream alive.

By 1950, Slick Airways had twenty-one planes hauling 2.5 million ton-miles over a route that included fifty-four cities in the United States; but it was suffering financially. In 1954 a merger with another freight carrier, the Flying Tiger Line, looked promising; and both companies were disappointed when the deal collapsed over branding issues.

For a period in the late 1950s the airline shut down its operations; and rumors persist that the planes were used for covert CIA (then OSS) operations until the company resumed its flights in 1962. There is documentation, with portions classified, that a Slick Airways plane landed at an Arizona military base in May, 1962, a time when the airline was supposedly suspended. In 1968 the company was acquired by Airlift International, and used mainly to fly the wounded and dead back from a new war underway in Vietnam. Aviation buffs still recall that cargo planes were a novel idea dreamed up by two brothers named Slick.

Meanwhile, operations on the ground were booming; and in 1947, Slick purchased the Benedum Field from one of his father's competitors, Michael Benedum, for $250,000. The risk paid off, and it became one of the largest post-World War II oil discoveries in the country; later yielding Slick a sales price of $2 million, which would be worth approximately ten times that today, with inflation.

That same year, Slick founded two more institutions that he was sure would move forward his dream of a "Science City" where diverse research would yield discoveries and applications to improve the world.

Southwest Research Institute was envisioned as an applied research facility that would work closely with the Foundation, his first creation, eventually helping to support its basic research once lucrative government contracts were secured.

Located next door to the Foundation, the Institute shared laboratory facilities and scientists in its early days; and close collaborations continued for more than thirty years, long after it became the third largest applied research organization in the United States.

The Institute of Inventive Research (IIR) was established to encourage creativity by inviting inventors to submit their ideas or products. It was housed in a barn at ESSAR Ranch; and in its first year of operation, Slick received more than five hundred letters and several hundred sample inventions, ranging from hair drying hoods that could be used at home, to a seamless tin can that while not particularly useful, was quite fascinating.

Slick was very active in managing all three of his institutions in their early years, making strategic decisions and engaging in long-range planning. By 1948, he recognized that growth of the three organizations had created new leadership demands; and a national search began for a scientist/president.

Dr. Harold Vagtborg was working as the director of research at the Armour Research Foundation in Chicago, Illinois, when Slick discovered him. Recognizing that the talented scientist and administrator might be attracted by the opportunity to lead an organization, rather than be in middle management at Armour, Slick pursued him with his usual force; and Vagtborg moved to Texas that fall.

With qualified hands-on management in place, Slick increased his traveling, continuing to funnel a constant flow of ideas for research projects, fundraising schemes, and potentially important contacts for the scientific institutes to Vagtborg from all over the world.

Between large amounts of time dreaming up scientific projects, considering ideas for new inventions, drilling for oil, running an airline, ranching and traveling to exotic places, not much time was spent at home. Despite a cozy home in the charming Monte Vista area of San Antonio, and young children, Slick's wife Polly felt isolated and alone. The fairytale marriage was experiencing some strain; and Polly began to resent being "molded into the perfect wife." Years later, Nixon family members would sigh ruefully, and comment that Nixons could never be molded.

With the same bursts of energy he gave every new venture, Slick made the most of every minute he shared with his children. He planned adventures at the Texas Coast and sophisticated outings to see the Rockettes in New York. He scoured catalogues to find amazing toys like gasoline-powered Model-T cars for the boys, and Patty's playhouse with a real doorbell and stove. He played with his children and their toys with absolute delight. He was the first in the neighborhood to introduce the brand new concept of Christmas lights in the yard – creating a life-size Santa Claus, sleigh, and reindeers that drew spectators from all over town.

Although oldest son William (nicknamed Bill by Slick, and called 'Wid' by his younger siblings) lived in Dallas with his mother, Slick's letters to his young son were constant and consistent, encouraging him in his studies, urging him to join in summer vacations, and trying to make the difficult environment that divorce creates more tolerable. All four children – Wid, Patty, Tom, and Chuck – established close bonds to each other, remained intensely loyal to their father, and much like the generation before, learned to enjoy the moments of togetherness and to survive the lonelier times.

While Slick wrote to his children about his exotic adventures – much the way his father had shared his gypsy life in the oilfields – he included Travis Richardson and a few other members of his inner circle in the journeys he made and the discoveries they produced.

"Tom would go off on a trip," Dorothy Richardson explains, "and we'd get a magazine all rolled up with grass seeds. Sometimes bugs would crawl out; and I'd have to burn the whole thing.

"Sometimes the seeds would be pristine; and we made some wonderful advances in grassland innovations in collaboration with the King Ranch."

After a trip to India in 1949, he contacted Richard Kleberg, who was both a family friend and the patriarch of the famous King Ranch, at that time the largest ranch in the world with more than one million fenced acres. He'd seen some plants and grasses on the other side of the world that he thought might be perfect of Texas and other parts of the U.S. that are hot and dry, and suggested that the King Ranch might test them after the agriculture division of the new Southwest Foundation had completed its research.

In addition to their shared interests in cattle and pasture development, Slick and Kleberg both intrigued by a ranch that was for sale in Cuba, in the early 1950s. Owned by an American woman whose husband had recently died; the ranch was reported to be incredibly beautiful.

"Tom wanted to look at a ranch in Cuba – right before Castro took over – and he wanted me to run it if he bought it. I told him I didn't want to move there," Richardson recalls. "But I traveled with him to look at it; and I understood his interest. It was beautiful land, with an older American widow, in debt, needing rescue. It had all the elements of a 'Tom Slick Adventure.'"

～

The single engine Cessna was low on gas, but re-fueling in Miami would not be possible. Flights to Cuba in 1950 were not encouraged; the U.S. State Department was aware of the activities of the *comunistas* and everyone knew that Fidel Castro was mounting troops for a revolution.

"Can we make it to Havana?" Tom Slick asked.

The small group of travelers was quiet as they waited for pilot Jack Barber's response. Slick was flying to Cuba with his ranch foreman and wife, Travis and Dorothy Richardson, to look at a ranch that was for sale on the eastern side of the island. The pilot hesitantly told the passengers that it would be close. Barring headwinds, they would probably make it without refueling. "Great!" Slick replied. "Let's keep going."

Richardson, now in his late seventies and still a rancher, remembered the landing as "hostile."

"No one was glad to see us," he recalled, "and the airport officials wanted us to turn around and go back home. But Tom just stepped off the plane smiling, made a few phone calls, and pretty soon we were all drinking *Cuba Libres* with the airport soldiers."

Slick's children saw their father work this magic many times. "My Dad had an amazing ability to get things done," his youngest son Chuck explained. "He just did not understand – or listen to – the word 'no.' If anyone said something could not be done, Dad would try it.

"As children, Patty, Tom and I would try to figure out how he could make a few phone calls and have tickets to a sold-out play, or dinner reservations someplace that needed to be booked weeks in advance. And everyone in the 'transaction' always seemed to be smiling. I'm still trying to figure it out!"

Whether it was securing special tickets to Disneyland for his children, or landing in Havana when the airport was officially closed, Slick believed that most 'no's' could be overcome. Sometimes he used charm; sometimes he used cash; sometimes he used a special magic that his friends all talk about; sometimes he used a combination of all of these ingredients to get what he wanted.

In Cuba, he wanted adventure and possibly a new ranch. After stocking up on supplies and hiring two native guides, Slick and the Richardsons traveled in a battered jeep to the far side of the island. The comunistas were patrolling the countryside, blowing into conch shells to send messages across the lush Cuban valleys. Richardson was aware of the drama about to unfold amidst the tall coconut orchards and tobacco plantations, far from Havana's elegant architecture and glamorous nightlife.

The rainy season had destroyed most of the dirt roads; the jungle vines and thick foliage had to be hacked back by Cuban workers wielding machetes; it was hot and humid. Every so often, Slick and the Richardsons stopped for refreshment.

"I'd chop down a coconut, and Dorothy would drink most of the milk inside," Richard remembered. "Then Tom would pour rum into the shell and the men would sip our own version of *piña coladas.*"

The ranch was beautiful, owned by a family friend of Slick's who had recently been widowed and wanted to move back to the United States. The spectacular ocean view, the lush grasses that would make wonderful grazing land for cattle, and a "woman in distress" were all factors in Slick's decision to buy it. But Richardson balked at the prospect of moving to Cuba in 1950 to run a new ranch; and he urged Slick not to purchase it.

"Tom was disappointed," Richardson said, "especially when the King Ranch decided to make the deal. They took horses and cattle over there and set up quite an operation. A few years later, Cuba took it all. Then I was a hero," Richardson laughed.

With the outbreak of World War II in the Pacific, Tom Slick volunteered for naval duty; but poor eyesight disqualified him. He served with the War Production Board in Washington, D.C. until 1943, when restrictions lessened and he was allowed to join the Navy, serving until 1945. (*Margaret Urschel Photo Collection.*)

Tom Slick and Bob West, who ran Slick's oil operations, experimented with various pistons and drilling bit inventions that they hoped would meet the challenge of the unusual drilling conditions in the famous Benedum Field. (*Tom Slick Photo Collection.*)

Travis Richardson was hired to oversee Slick's ranching operations in 1946; he helped develop the Brangus breed of cattle and participated in many Slick adventures. (*Travis Richardson Photo Collection.*)

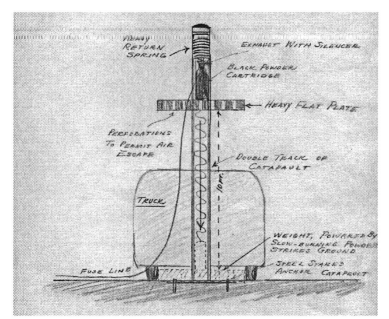

Tom Slick's sketch of an idea for a new truck and catapult system designed to conduct seismic testing with a minimum of noise. (*Tom Slick Collection.*)

Tom Slick, c. 1941. (*Courtesy of Southwest Foundation Photo Archives.*)

The Cable House, purchased as part of Slick's new ESSAR Ranch in 1940, became the home of his first scientific institutes, as well as his personal residence. (*Photos courtesy of Southwest Foundation for Biomedical Research and Southwest Research Institute.*)

Miss Polly Nixon
To Wed T.B. Slick

Polly Nixon was young, beautiful and accomplished; but the fairytale aura to her marriage to Tom Slick would not last. (*Wedding Engagement Announcement photo, June 1946, courtesy of* San Antonio Express-News.)

Close family ties: Berenice Urschel, with brother-in-law and sister, Arthur and Ramona Seeligson, whose son would eventually marry Polly Nixon's sister. (*Ramona Seeligson Photo Collection.*)

81

Earl Slick founded Slick Airways in 1946, with older brother Tom, brother-in-law Lew Moorman, and Charles Urschel, Jr., as partners. (*Photo courtesy of The Mind Science Foundation Photo Collection.*)

Slick Airways was established by Earl Slick in 1946, in partnership with Tom Slick and Lew Moorman. The idea of an airline devoted to freight was innovative and launched a new concept in aviation history. (*Betty Slick Moorman Photo Collection.*)

Slick Airlines introduced the idea of a cargo-focused business to aviation. (*Betty Slick Moorman Photo Collection*)

Tom Slick's airplane, c. 1950.

In 1950, a beautiful widow in distress lured Tom Slick, Travis and Dorothy Richardson to Cuba to explore buying her ranch. The flight was memorable. (*Travis Richardson Photo Collection.*)

In the Cuban jungles, the Tom Slick expedition found a way to make "Cuba Libres," c. 1950. (*Travis Richardson Photo Collection.*)

Chapter Five

Slick Ideas
(1950 – 1955)

He addressed the letter to "The Indian Government, New Delhi, India," added an airmail stamp, and waited for an answer. Tom Slick never considered that the rather vague address, or possible security issues, might interfere with the delivery of his hand-written note:

> *Dear Sirs:*
>
> *My attention has been called to a newspaper article giving some information on a specially devised box to send spawns of fish alive by air to distant places.*
>
> *I am interested in getting some spawn of Monsoor? (spelling?) fish from India if you think it feasible and if they can be transplanted in the United States.*
>
> *Any information you can give me on this matter will be greatly appreciated.*
>
>

Very truly yours,
Tom Slick

A few weeks later, an official-looking envelope covered in Indian stamps was waiting on his desk; the information he had requested had arrived; and he began to arrange to bring the famous fighting fish of the Ganges to the Guadalupe River in Texas.

A voracious reader, especially of newspapers and magazines, Slick always turned pages with his imagination at full throttle. He searched for anything new or controversial, and made quick mental leaps to ways the information might be applied to his scientific research programs, livestock and ranching business, oil ventures, interest in world peace, or some exciting new gift for his young children.

Slick wrote to President Dwight Eisenhower about the need for the United States to remain on the cutting edge of technology internationally, to Aristotle Onassis about tankers, to Norman Cousins, David Rockefeller, and Secretary of State John Foster Dulles about world peace, to construction powerhouse George Brown about building a floating recreation center in New York's east river, and to oilmen Clint Murchison and Sid Richardson about an even more valuable natural resource – water. He knew some of these powerful men personally, but some were total strangers. He never hesitated to contact anybody, with any idea. His wealth certainly contributed to his confidence that those he contacted would respond; but there was more to it than that. He'd learned from his father, Lucky Tom, that "nothing ventured meant nothing gained," whether it was prospecting for oil or making a telephone call.

In 1954, Slick bought a plantation in Mississippi and began to think of crops and livestock that might be introduced there. After a hunting and fishing trip to New Zealand that summer, he wrote to a rancher downunder to inquire about the possibility of bringing Romney Marsh sheep to the United States, explaining that "it would be interesting to try them out in this country, and if successful, build up some sort of popularity in the breed." He asked S.C. Sutherland to send him three rams and six ewes, adding that "we would also like to breed up some Cordales or some other type of starting stock. We would want them for meat as well as wool, with meat being perhaps more important than wool in this country. I would appreciate your thoughts."

He became interested in an inventor who claimed to have developed a men's hair tonic that could change the direction that hair grew. His brother-in-law, Jim Nixon, remembers it was an appealing idea in the 1950s, when men coated their hair with thick balms like "Lucky Tiger" to force unruly cowlicks into the smooth, slicked-back look of the times.

Slick found an article about a "Four-in-One Trailer" in the June, 1955 issue of *Popular Mechanics* and immediately wrote to the manufacturer in West Virginia for details about its ability to function as a raft, boat trailer, and camper. That same year, he ordered a pair of skunks, that had no scent glands, as an interesting holiday surprise for his sons, Tom and Chuck. Their unique pets added tremendously to their popularity that year.

Slick put equal thought and energy into gifts for his wife, Polly. In 1954, he wrote directly to Stanley Marcus, the CEO of Neiman Marcus, then the most elegant department store in Texas (which would expand nationally in the 1980s), asking him to help find a perfect gift for her birthday. Ironically, one of his ideas was a set of beautiful luggage, "blue and green plaid," so she would be equipped to travel on some of the adventures he was planning.

Later that year, the couple appeared in *Time Magazine*, in a photo with U.S. President Eisenhower. All are smiling and look happy, but the facts were different.

The model of marriage that had worked for his mother and father in the early 1900s was not as successful for Tom Slick nearly fifty years later. While his children accepted his absences and enjoyed the adventures they shared together (as Tom and Betty had done with their father), Polly Slick expected more. In 1955 they divorced amicably; and they remained good friends for the rest of Slick's life. Eventually she remarried; and at times, she and her new husband, Paul Pater, the three children, and Slick would have dinner together. All recognized a complex, important bond, and took special care to maintain it.

With the change in his home life, Slick allocated even more time to his research institutes and new technologies in the oil business. In 1955 he met Robert West, Jr., a young man who had just earned his doctorate in Chemical Engineering from the University of Texas. Slick liked West's combination of academic expertise, practical know-how, and creativity, and offered him the job of running Slick Oil. Nearly fifty years later, West smiled as he remembered telling Slick that despite his strengths in related fields, he did not have experience in the oil business. He was hired immediately. It's another example of the intuitive hiring practices he used, based more on people than anything else. West went on to supervise innovative new secondary oil recovery processes and other pioneering technologies, and eventually he built the oil company (renaming it

Tesoro after Slick's death) into the first Texas company to be listed on the New York stock exchange, eventually valued at forty-two billion dollars.

After more than a decade of existence, Slick's scientific research organizations were beginning to thrive. The first oral contraceptives developed at Southwest Foundation were proving successful and plans were underway to develop a new primate research colony.

With Vagtborg in place as a fulltime director of Southwest Foundation, Southwest Research Institute, and the Institute of Inventive Research, Slick encouraged him to build a management team. In 1955 Martin Goland, an aerospace engineer employed by Midwest Research Institute, in Kansas City, Missouri, was hired to head the Institute's technical program. Goland convinced Hungarian engineer Stephen Juhasz to join the migration south as well; and his expertise in fossil fuels research and heat transfer soon elevated SwRI to new levels of engineering. Juhasz, in his nineties in 2001, remembered that the "staff directory filled an entire page, we had two hundred employees" (about 10 percent of the Institute's current ranks).

Scientists and inventors who were in the laboratories during the late 1940s and early 1950s, remember many "Slick ideas," and the overall spirit of open-mindedness and creativity that was so important to their boss.

"Tom Slick believed that people and ideas were more important than bricks and mortar," seventy-five-year-old Bill Mallow, a materials scientist and inventor at Southwest Research Institute for more than forty years, said in 2001. "He would stop by my office, and the visit never ended without at least a dozen new twists to what I was working on, and usually some thoughts on what I might do next."

Mallow went on to find the right chemical ingredients for "Liquid Paper," a secretary's idea for correcting typing mistakes, and invented a special soil additive to reduce the formation of "potholes" in aging roads. He also worked briefly on Slick's artificial pecans project.

When Slick realized that a drought in Texas, where most commercial pecans are grown, would impact the cost of the precious nuts, he suggested that scientists at Southwest Research Institute should invent an artificially flavored "pecan," without a shell (since shelling also raised the cost of the natural nuts), that would be an economic alternative for the baking industry.

After about a year of careful mixing, and work on color, consistency and flavor, the artificial nuts were ready to market. But a drought-free year produced a bumper crop of real pecans and a new shelling device brought their cost down still more. That year, most of the artificial pecans found their way into holiday baskets at the Institute, along with turkeys, jalapeno jellies, champagne and other delicacies that Tom Slick gave his employees and friends during the Christmas season. "They would be an odd, but precious, souvenir today," Mallow concluded with a chuckle, "but of course everyone used them to bake cookies during their brief existence."

Slick enjoyed ideas and liked people who had lots of them. Some of his more conservative friends often warned him that he was too open, making him vulnerable to opportunists, he countered with his own views about discovery.

"I always believe in taking a positive approach, instead of a negative one where everyone just sits back and says that everything inconclusive is impossible," he said in 1952. The frontiers of possibility were where Slick preferred to spend his time; and he never hesitated to give any person or idea his thoughtful attention, however far from traditional thinking or so-called proven science it took him.

"I have found that in many cases highly trained technical men are not willing to even look at claims that are beyond known technical theory," he said, "and I'm convinced that some of the most important advances will come from accidental discoveries."

Through both Southwest Foundation and the Institute of Inventive Research, Slick received thousands of ideas – some scientific and very exciting, some totally unscientific and also very exciting. He loved the profound science behind an idea that arrived in 1954 from Dr. Harlow Shapley at the Harvard College Observatory, suggesting a design for an electronic telescope, which would convert light to electrons, multiplying and converting back to light. A similar concept found practical application when Westinghouse developed and marketed an x-ray image intensifier.

That same summer, Slick wrote to the Woods Hole Oceanography Institute to learn more about their new device to measure the speed and direction of ocean currents while a ship was moving. "I was wondering if the same instrument could give you a true ground speed indicator in an airplane, for which it seems to me there is a very great need," he told the research group, offering to explore a cooperative development between the Woods Hole institute and the Institute of Inventive Research.

The 1950s produced extraordinary ideas and inventions that are such an accepted part of today's twenty-first century life that it is difficult to imagine how remarkable they were at the time. In 1953, AT&T began to lay the first telephone cable across the Atlantic ocean; and new refrigeration technologies made it possible to develop a home freezer. Long distance telephone service and frozen foods were novel ideas.

Slick tracked as many marvelous inventions as he could, linking many to the four research institutes he had founded over the past decade. Each one was part of Slick's overall vision of a "Science City"; and like siblings, each organization had its role in the family. First born, Southwest Foundation was chartered to conduct basic research. Its early work produced new discoveries in agriculture and livestock breeding, including new drought-resistant grasses and artificial insemination; and breakthroughs in medicine, including oral contraceptives, new treatments for heart disease, important advances in genetics, and most recently vaccines for infectious diseases like Hepatitis A and B.

Slick was a very young man – just twenty-five years old – when he "fathered" this first scientific foundation, and he remained especially proud of it throughout his life. A few scientists from its earliest days remember how different scientific research was at ESSAR in the 1950s.

"After completing a Fulbright Scholarship at Rochester Medical Center in New York in 1954, I returned to my home in southern India," Dr. Pemmaraju N. Rao explained nearly fifty years later, gazing towards the multi-million dollar biocontainment laboratory this is visible just outside his office window at the Southwest Foundation tor Biomedical Research, contemplating the changes he has seen in the surroundings during more than four decades. A letter from Dr. Leonard Axelrod, a colleague at Rochester, urged him to come back to the United States to work with him at a new research facility in Texas.

"When I arrived in 1956 from India, I discovered a ranch house in the middle of nowhere; and I was totally shocked," the veteran scientist laughed. But complete scientific freedom and the confidence that emanated from Tom Slick, along with the promise of more modern facilities soon, were enough to keep the Foundation's first small staff of six scientists passionately at work in their somewhat "wild west" setting..

Rao and colleague Leonard Axelrod made important discoveries in steroid research, which eventually led to new understanding about hormone metabolism, its link to cancer, and some of the anti-hormones used today to treat breast cancer, and other tumor inhibitors.

Rao remembers finding a snake in his laboratory refrigerator, and Joseph Goldzieher, one of the world's pioneers in contraception and reproduction research, recalls that his un-airconditioned work space was so hot that his team had to work at night to avoid being anesthetized by the ether they were using in their experiments. Both men agree that Tom Slick's offer of total freedom was more appealing than the state-of-the-art facilities they might have had elsewhere.

Goldzieher was a 1940 graduate from Harvard University, and received his medical degree from New York University College of Medicine. He has balanced a private medical practice, teaching and research for more than fifty years, and has received numerous awards for his discoveries, most notably the development of oral and injectable hormonal contraceptives.

Slick was convinced that population control could offer the world an important opportunity for breaking the cycles of poverty and conflict; Goldzieher remembers their conversations about the positive impact of contraception and family planning long before the topic gained any public awareness. During trips to Africa, India, and other developing nations in the late 1950s, Slick always mentioned the work underway at Southwest Foundation with pride and an optimistic confidence that it would make a positive difference in world economies. Decades later Goldzieher has seen his discoveries in endocrinology and hormone research honored by organizations around the globe, including the Women's Health Initiative; and today oral contraception methods are practiced around the world.

"Tom Slick was interested in me because I was from India," Rao said with a smile. "He was fascinated by the mystical aspects of life; and by 1958, he had visited India, Tibet, Nepal and Bhutan. We had great conversations about paranormal phenomena and he was organizing a new scientific institute to study them."

The Mind Science Foundation was established in late 1958; and in 2005, Dr. Pemmaraju Rao is one of its most respected Board members. Still an active scientist at Southwest Foundation for Biomedical Research, Rao, like Slick, has dedicated his life to scientific discovery, without ignoring those mysteries that may not always have a scientific explanation.

About the same time that Rao, Alexrod, and Goldzieher arrived in Texas to work at the Foundation, Slick met a Harvard Business School graduate named Bill Rhame, through mutual friends in New York. Rhame had graduated in record time, with honors; and Slick was impressed by his intelligence, clever wit, and readiness to take risks in the business world. Deciding he would be a perfect manager for his multi-faceted business interests, Slick lured him to San Antonio as well, organizing Texstar Corporation as a holding company for all of his endeavors, and making Rhame its new president.

Later that year, Slick's sister, Betty Moorman, suggested an innovative way to raise money for her brother's favorite research facility, and Rhame assisted with the rather tricky financial planning. Jesse Oppenheimer, a family friend and respected attorney, added his expertise to the evolving idea that eventually would provide more than $650,000 in annual contributions to Southwest Foundation.

Moorman gathered her best friends and asked them to help her design a unique and exclusive dining club, where all dues and profits would go towards supporting research at the Foundation. The city's most elegant hostesses joined forces with the sharpest legal and business minds; and The Argyle Club was born in 1956.

Located on a quiet street in one of San Antonio's most beautiful residential areas, the club had once been a boarding house and a bakery. Its southern charm includes a magnificent lawn and garden, an old-fashioned veranda framed by high colonial pillars, a number of intimate dining areas, and a long waiting list for membership.

Oppenheimer's creative legal thinking produced a plan that would enable a club to be established to support the Foundation, built with tax deductible funds. The old boarding house was purchased for $32,203; a renovation plan was designed; and a membership plan that was advantageous to its members as well as the Foundation was created. A hearing was held at the IRS in Washington, DC, since the plan was so innovative; and Oppenheimer was successful in his negotiations to establish the Argyle as a 501(c).4 entity.

Oppenheimer was on the Club's first Board of Directors, along with Moorman, Rhame, and other civic leaders including socialites Peggy Becker and Elizabeth Urschel, banker Tom Frost, and arts patron Margaret Tobin. His recollections of early meetings with some of the city's first members include decisions to furnish the Club with "extra things" stored in their own attics, and the first Christmas party at the Argyle in 1957 was a huge success.

"I learned an important lesson for the future," Oppenheimer remembers with a smile. "As we went around the Board table, voting on whether or not to have a party, each person said, 'Oh, no … there's too much going on at Christmas and the last thing we need is another party to go to.'

"When we got around to Peggy Becker, she rolled her eyes and in her very appealing way said, 'Charlie and I don't have too much to do at Christmas time. We have said no so many times that we don't get to say no anymore!'

"Her statement has guided me in many situations," Oppenheimer says, adding that he never heard Tom Slick say 'no' either.

Today, other non-profits around the country have followed the Club's innovative fund-raising model, impressed that donations received from the Argyle equal an amount close to the income generated by an endowment of $50 million or more.

Slick was a tireless fundraiser too. He wrote to his family, friends, and complete strangers, urging them to support his first research venture. Like a proud father, he listed its accomplishments and shared his dreams for its maturity. In a letter to his mother, Berenice Urschel, Slick explained the new changes in tax law as positive for charitable giving, and used the "matching grant" idea, urging her to match her brother-in-law, Arthur Seeligson's year-end contribution in 1957:

"Old Arthur, who as you know is plenty smart about taxes, and throws money away just like glue, has offered to give the Foundation $12,000. This is about as strong a recommendation that it makes money for him as I can think of."

Still another innovative fundraising strategy emerged in the form of memorial gifts. Today, contributions made to a nonprofit organization to honor a family member or friend who has died are very common; in the 1950s, they were controversial, viewed by some as inappropriate. Flower merchants were especially critical of this new "competition"; but the Southwest Foundation promoted the memorials as more meaningful.

In a letter defending the Foundation's position, Slick admits that "my personal feeling is that every expense connected with funerals is a great waste which should be put to more constructive purposes … I feel very strongly about it, as I have seen some cases where people who very badly needed the money were talked into spending it on useless funeral expenses at a time when their sales resistance was low…for me, flowers are something that should be used for happiness and happy occasions. For a memorial … I personally cannot help preferring something more constructive."

Despite his strong defense of the new program, he was sensitive to how others might feel, and was careful to say often that preferences always are personal and should be honored as such.

His attention to personal preferences also extended to Slick's hiring practices. He believed that finding the right people for any job was the real key to future success; and he used a special "technique" to lure the very best to his team. He called it "the red car" offer.

To attract the scientists, oilmen, ranchers, businessmen, and others who joined Slick's different endeavors, he first gave serious thought to each candidate's particular personality and desires, understanding that every human being is unique, with specific needs and hopes. When Slick discovered that mystery in each potential employee, he offered the very thing that made the job irresistible. Sometimes the lure might really be a red car; but usually it was something less tangible and more meaningful.

In ranch foreman Travis Richardson's case, it was the opportunity to realize his longtime dream of running a cattle operation. In chemical engineer Bob West's case, it was the challenge of hands-on experience in the oil business and innovative experimenting with new recovery methods. In Dr. Harold Vagtborg's case, it was the chance to be the man in charge of a new research endeavor, rather than be "number two" at a more established laboratory, in Bill Rhame's case, it was the opportunity to combine business with extremely creative risk-taking.

Slick had an unusual sensitivity to dreams and longings, both his own and those of others. When he found human talent and spirit that he liked, he often re-shaped the job description to add that person to his team.

It did not always work. Both of his wives possessed the talent and spirit he liked; and they were intelligent and beautiful as well. But neither could adapt to the "re-shaped job description" that was part of marriage to Tom Slick. While he tried to satisfy their dreams of a conventional home life, his own dreams bubbled up from a deep well of curiosity about the world; and exotic people, out-of-the box ideas, and mystic landscapes danced in Tom Slick's mind. New rumors of a diamond pipeline in the Amazon jungle, and separate reports of a shaman's extraordinary abilities were about to lure the mystery hunter away from home again.

Tom Slick suggested that Southwest Foundation establish a baboon research colony; today it houses the largest population of baboons in the world. (*Photo courtesy of Southwest Foundation for Biomedical Research.*)

William T. Rhame, a "whiz kid" Harvard Business School graduate, was hired by Slick in 1955 to manage Texstar Corporation, a holding company for a growing number of "Slick ideas." (*Fred Rhame Photo Collection.*)

Working with Travis Richardson and the University of Louisiana, Tom Slick was sure that the new Brangus breed of cattle would prove optimal for the hot, dry climate in Texas. (*Photo courtesy of the Mind Science Foundation.*)

Tom Slick and Harold Vagtborg, the first director of Slick's scientific research institutes, c. 1949. (*Southwest Foundation for Biomedical Research Photo Collection.*)

Bill Rhame, Betty Slick Moorman, and Tom Slick launched the Argyle Club in 1955 as an innovative way to raise money for scientific research underway at Southwest Foundation. (*Betty Slick Moorman Photo Collection.*)

The Argyle Club was established by Betty Slick Moorman in 1956 as an innovative way to raise money for Slick's Southwest Foundation. The Club's profits, along with annual contributions made by its members support scientific research. (*Photo courtesy of The Argyle.*)

In 1954, Tom Slick's cousin Arthur Seeligson, Jr., married Linda Nixon, youngest sister of Tom's wife Polly. Polly Nixon Slick is pictured on the far right, next to her twin sister, Patty Nixon Taliaferro. (*Ramona Seeligson Photo Collection.*)

The bride's mother, Mrs. James W. Nixon (Julie), and the groom's mother, Mrs. Arthur Seeligson (Ramona) were already close friends when their children married. (*Ramona Seeligson Photo Collection.*)

Chapter Six

Diamonds and Death
(1954 – 1956)

In the spring of 1954, Tom Slick met an adventurer named Leonard Clark in San Francisco. The two discussed their shared interest in exploration, and Clark gave Slick a manuscript describing conditions in the Amazon region of South America, where Slick thought there was potential for oil exploration. Soon after the meeting, Clark wrote to Slick, inviting him to participate in an expedition to British Guiana (now Guyana) in the Amazon to investigate oil indications, mineral deposits, and Indian medicines used by native *curanderos*.

Although not able to accompany Clark, Slick was intrigued and wrote back about the Indian medicines with enthusiasm.

"If you find any medicines that seem to be good, be sure to bring out sizable samples so that we can have our scientists confirm their effectiveness. Also, if you find any oil seeps, bring out some bottle samples together with careful descriptions and locations."
Letter from Tom Slick to Leonard Clark
April 26, 1954

Slick explained that while Clark would be on expedition in South America, he would be in India studying "the superior control of the mind which they claim the Indians have achieved", followed by a journey to the Himalayas to investigate reports of the "abominable snow men."

The following year, Clark sent Slick a copy of *Diamonds, Gold and Orchids*, by William Lavarre. Clark knew Lavarre slightly, and was interested in his claim to have discovered a "diamond pipeline" in South America. Slick read the book, and sent it on to Bob Kleberg, a close friend, and the owner of the famous King Ranch, then the largest ranch in the world. For once, Slick was a bit skeptical, noting that "this fellow certainly writes an interesting adventure story which he tells me is true … it is a little hard to believe in some of the details."

Leonard Clark continued to correspond with Slick, sending him reports of intriguing discoveries, and with time, Slick's curiosity overcame his skepticism.

In 1956 he organized his British Guiana Expedition with a budget of $13,000. The diamond-hunting team included Slick, who would contribute $10,500 of the funds needed, Ted Macklin, an associate of Leonard Clark's from California, who would contribute $2,500, Leonard Clark, who would serve as Expedition Field Leader and be paid $500 a month for two months, Macklin's son Dick, who would serve as Deputy Field Leader and be paid similarly, Dr. Mather, a geologist on leave from Southwest Research Institute, who would be paid his regular salary, and the pilot of the private plane that would transport the team and its equipment and supplies to South America.

As the departure, planned for early November, 1956, approached, Slick decided to add another team member – his ranch foreman, Travis Richardson. Explaining that he was "a tough young fellow, a good shot, and someone I trust," Slick knew he would add common sense to the expedition, and that he could investigate South American ranching opportunities during the same trip.

Slick would fly commercially to Buenos Aires and Rio de Janeiro on private business, then on to Caracas to join the rest of the expedition team, which was scheduled to fly straight from Texas to Venezuela.

"Our plane from San Antonio to South America had guns and ammo and equipment, but no permit," Travis Richardson recalls. "We made it to Maricaibo, where we were grounded and the plane was sealed. I begged them to hold the plane 'in transit' while I flew to Caracas to meet Tom and tell him what had happened.

"Once I found Tom in Caracas, he made a few phone calls, and everything was fine. The grounded plane in Maricaibo got clearance and flew on to Georgetown, British Guiana. Tom and I met the rest of the group there, and we got ready to go into the jungle."

Georgetown was a wild place in 1956, much like the gold rush towns of California and Colorado a century before. Richardson remembers that it was filled with adventurers looking for diamonds, gold, or any other business that might mean money.

"I remember one young man from New York City was in Georgetown, said he was in the diamond business, asked me who our expedition's 'money man' was. That was an interesting thing about Tom – he always blended in with everyone else; no one ever knew that he was a millionaire."

The team went deep into the jungle; and Slick was as excited as a small boy at Christmas time as he collected samples of natural herbal medicines and cures from the Indians. While Slick enthusiastically courted the shamans, urging them to share their secrets, others on the expedition were not as trusting. The men took turns keeping a watch, sleeping every other night, not at all certain what these foreign men dressed in loincloths might do. "It was like the movies," Richardson says. "The men had painted their faces and bodies and were very vain; the women were plain-looking and seemed to do all the work."

The search for the "diamond pipeline" was not as successful as the investigation of traditional medicine, but Slick's enthusiasm was not deterred. He was sure that Clark and Macklin would find the mystical place described in Lavarre's book, *Diamonds, Gold & Orchids*, where the natural rock and soil conditions created an unnatural "pipe" for the formation of the precious stones. They would stay on in British Guiana, exploring the jungle, while Slick, Richardson, and the geologist Mather would return to the United States.

"When we came back from our first jungle search for the pipeline, the diamond salesman from New York was still in Georgetown, talking about a gold deal. Tom had to get back to Texas, so he didn't bite, otherwise he might have. That was always a danger ... he was curious about everything."

Getting back to Texas did not prove simple. The plane would have to make two flights from Georgetown to Caracas since not all the team members and equipment could fly in the plane at one time. As the first flight took off from the grass strip, the plane's wings dipped dangerously and it was obvious to everyone on the ground that something was terribly wrong. An experienced pilot, Jack Barber realized that he had engine trouble and tried to bring the plane back down, crashing into one of the giant anthills that stood several feet tall on the turf just beyond the airstrip. No one was hurt, but the plane was badly damaged.

Richardson, scheduled to go on the second flight, was on the ground and watched in horror as the plane with Tom Slick aboard crashed to the ground. Later, he would ask if his boss if he'd been frightened. "The answer was 'no'," Richardson says. "Tom explained that he believed in predestination, which really makes fear nonexistent."

According to some friends who remember the South American airplane crash, the U.S. State Department had warned Slick that there was a lot of Russian activity in British Guiana; some believe that sabotage may have been the cause of the crash on the grass air strip in Georgetown. The engine only had 291 hours on it and the plane had been completely serviced before it left Brownsville, Texas.

By the end of 1956, Slick and Richardson were back in Texas, but Macklin and Clark continued to hunt for the diamond pipeline, and now gold as well, re-naming the expedition the *Polvo de Oro* (Gold Dust). They kept Slick apprised of their adventures, but by early 1957, the "money man" was ready to close down the operation. He wrote to his explorers, praising them for their hard work and expressing some disappointment in William Lavarre's character and published accounts of the pipeline.

"...Sounds like you've had some real adventures. I was proud to hear that you were able to follow the deductions of Ted (Macklin), but of course it was disappointing that you found nothing at the final site. I don't know if Lavarre is just a liar or what. We have been trying to contact him since my return but so far have not been able to get in touch with him.

...we had better cross off that part of the project."
Letter to Dick Macklin and Leonard Clark, January 7, 1957

The letter continues for five pages, outlining all sorts of other potential deals that Slick was developing in South America. He continued to pay Macklin and Clark to be his "scouts", and instructed them to further investigate the gold property deal (*Polvo de Oro*), as well as to follow up on the salvage efforts for the crashed airplane and to check into partnership potential in a proposed air service trading company that was being developed in British Guiana.

Macklin and Clark stayed another year carrying out these instructions, and exploring the jungles; then tragedy struck as they prepared to return to the United States at the end of 1957. As a last "holiday" adventure in the jungle they'd come to know well, the two young men decided to take a canoe trip down the ferocious Paraguay River. After a plane crash, jungle encounters with tribesmen who still practiced the art of shrinking the heads of their dead enemies, and a life-threatening snakebite, they felt their river trip would be an easy jaunt. The water volume was especially high that year, due to torrential rains; and their inexperience did not prepare them for the strong current that swept their canoe over the falls.

The deaths of Leonard Clark and Dick Macklin brought the South American operations to an end; and Tom Slick had the difficult job of contacting the young men's families and expressing the sadness and sympathy that he felt. His own experiences of loss, especially his father's death at a young age and its effects on his entire family, made Slick especially sensitive to grief. He was quick to call and offer sympathy; he followed up with thoughtful notes for many months; he put aside his disappointment that the Macklin/Clark manuscript from the South American endeavor was never recovered. As was his way, he turned his thoughts to the future, to ways he could introduce the Indian medicines to his scientific labs for study and to a way he could use the few diamonds from the Amazon to create something meaningful.

After two years of searching in the jungle of British Guiana, five small stones had been retrieved; one was an unusual greenish color. Slick asked Bob Haack, a jeweler in Wisconsin, to make a ring for his ten-year-old daughter, Patty, using the diamonds. His letter suggests that the jeweler use the green diamond in the center, and instructs him to make the ring "as simple but as effective as possible... something she could probably wear later on too." He added a postscript that Patty's birthday was approaching and asked that it be sent in time to surprise her. She never knew the underlying cost of those diamonds, but she treasured the ring, presented by a father who moved easily and often between adventures but always came home bearing gifts for the people he loved and the research efforts he championed.

From the Amazon, Tom Slick brought back jewels for his little girl, dart guns and a shrunken head for his sons, and a pet monkey for his brother, Earl. He also brought bundles of plants, vials of strange liquids, and stories collected from shamanic healers back to the Southwest Foundation where scientists would try to differentiate between magic and science.

"The difference between a poison, a medicine, and a narcotic is only one of dosage," Dr. Nixon said as he examined the samples Tom Slick's expedition team had collected in the rain forests of Guyana. Slick had seen firsthand the miraculous effect one medicinal plant had on a snake bite; the Indians had used delicate poison darts to hunt as effectively as any big game hunter; and the tiny, exquisite shrunken heads he brought back to Texas certainly were proof that the jungle shamans knew things that Western doctors did not.

After taking his specimens to the laboratory at Southwest Foundation, where scientists could study their chemical compositions, Slick invited his ex-father-in-law, Polly's father, Dr. James W. Nixon, to come see them. Nixon had earned one of the first medical degrees from the University of Pennsylvania in 1919, studied orthopedic medicine in Vienna, Austria, in 1920, and eventually practiced medicine in San Antonio for fifty years, retiring at the age of eighty. Unlike many Western physicians, he did not scoff at traditional medicine; in fact he had grown up with it and respected what it might teach the "modern world".

As a young boy, Nixon accompanied his father – a combination of country doctor and Texas rancher – on medical calls in a horse-drawn buggy. He never forgot that he'd seen homemade potions work as well as pills, or his father's willingness to listen to the *curanderos* who had learned "magical healing" in Mexico. He told Slick about an old *mestizo* who had arrived at the family ranch with a burro loaded with brush. The Indian claimed that the plants could cure diarrhea, which was a chronic problem in Texas and Mexico in the late 1800s. Nixon was a scientist at heart, and like the majority of the population in those days, also suffered from dysentery. He decided to experiment. Following the old man's advice, he brewed a tea from the *chaparro amargoso* ("bitter bush") and tested it on himself. Impressed by his miraculous cure, he sent the plants to London's finest pharmaceutical house, Sharp & Dohme; and in 1898, wrote the first treatise on a cure for amoebic dysentery. The curative compounds from bitter bush made drugs which are still used today.

As Nixon related this childhood memory to his ex-son-in-law, Slick felt his excitement mounting. While in British Guiana, he actually had tasted a variety of bitter bush. Late one afternoon, after the most remarkable fishing trip of his life (when large fish were caught by dainty poisoned darts, blown from the mouths of Indian fishermen maneuvering their canoes over rocks and rapids), Slick listened as the old shaman who had accompanied the expedition pointed to a thin bush, with gray bark and small red flowers, explaining that it was used to treat fevers and diarrhea. It was so bitter that Slick had followed it with a rum chaser, which he later learned was a century-old custom.

The curative powers of South American bitter bush were first documented during the colonial period, when a famous black medicine man escaped from a slave colony in British Guiana and managed to reach the Netherlands. He brought plants and herbs from the jungle with him; and his power to cure diarrhea caused by intestinal parasites soon was legendary. His most potent concoction was a tea made from "very bitter wood".

About the same time the country doctor from Texas was writing his treatise and introducing a cure for diarrhea in the southwestern United States, an escaped slave was introducing a South American version of "bitter bush" to Europe.

In British Guiana, patients soon learned that the very best delivery of the medicine occurred when a cup was carved from the bitter wood and filled with rum. The liquor absorbed the curative compounds from the wood; and the drink tasted far better than the bitter tea.

Slick was intrigued by ancient medicinal potions and healing rituals for several reasons, the simplest being his belief that modern medicine could learn from them. But his growing fascination with the untapped power of the human mind also led him to explore them as possible gateways to altered states of consciousness.

Natural hallucinogens were a part of many cultures in the remote places that Slick traveled. From the jungles of the Amazon to the Kalahari Desert, from the volcanic plateaus of Mexico and Central America to the high peaks of the Himalayas, Slick had interviewed healers about their "out of body" experiences, of transformations into jaguars, lions, flying tigers and other creatures, in order to travel more quickly through the more mysterious realms.

"How do you do it?" Slick wanted to know.

"You feel like the wind," a *curandero* in Veracruz told him. "I feel my lion-hair growing," a *Jul'hoansi* Bushman in Botswana explained. "It is like dying," a South American shaman said.

Facing one's own death comes up often as part of the rigorous training required to become a healer. And unlike Western civilization's avoidance of the subject, the mystic worlds embrace death as a part of life. Slick loved to discuss the subject with friends, often asking what they thought happened after death, always alert for new ideas on the subject.

Ethnobotanist and anthropologist Wade Davis, author of *The Serpent and the Rainbow, One River: Explorations and Discoveries in the Amazon Rain Forest,* and *Light at the Edge of the World* has spent nearly thirty years researching and writing about these topics, first as a student at Harvard, and currently as an Explorer-in-Residence at the National Geographic Society.

According to Davis, some of these mysteries can be dangerously potent, despite their tempting promise to take the curious "on a thousand flights of spirit."

Flights of spirit appealed to Slick; and he always wondered what was on the other side. So he didn't hesitate to taste the bitter concoctions he was offered in the jungle, but according to his diary, none transported him beyond his hammock.

Noting that the Amazon possesses more varieties of plants and animals than any other place on earth, Slick looked for the *curura*, a giant toad that weighs as much as seven pounds, and the incredible *capybara*, a rodent that weighs 120 pounds. But despite these exciting possibilities, hidden in the immense green canopy of jungle, another more elusive creature and reports of more mystical healing phenomena on the other side of the world had won Slick's ever-searching attention.

When he left his young adventurers, Dick Macklin and Leonard Clark in the Amazon, to collect as many medicinal specimens (and diamonds) as possible, he had shifted his focus to the Himalayas, where mysticism, magical healing, and the Abominable Snowman awaited him.

The South American country of Guyana was still British Guiana when Slick mounted his expedition to search for the "diamond pipeline."

Tom Slick in British Guiana, 1956. (*Travis Richardson Photo Collection.*)

112

Science or magic ... or both? Tom Slick was curious about healing ceremonies, and the altered states of consciousness that accompanied them. His experiences in British Guiana, India, and the Himalayas would eventually inspire him to start still another scientific institute to study these phenomena. (*Photos courtesy of the Mind Science Foundation.*)

Shamanic practices in the jungle fascinated Slick, who carried back local plant cures to be studied at his scientific institutes. (*Photo courtesy of the Mind Science Foundation.*)

Tom Slick in the laboratories at Southwest Foundation for Biomedical Research. (*Photo courtesy of the SFBR Photo Collection.*)

Even while exploring the jungles of British Guiana, Slick continued to dream about the creature his father had told him stories about in 1922. He carried an old copy of the French magazine Radar with him to South America, and told his expedition members that he was ready to search for "L'Homme des Neiges" (the Snowman) in the Himalayas.

115

Chapter Seven

The Search for the Yeti
(1955-1960)

O nly a *pukka shikari* (*true hunter*) will ever catch a Yeti," Tenzing Norgay, the world famous Sherpa who accompanied Sir Edmund Hillary to the top of Mt. Everest, told a group of near-frozen trekkers gathered around a blazing fire at Rathong Camp in Sikkim in the winter of 1956. He explained that the creature was always on the move and very cunning.

According to Tenzing, his father, a yak herder in Tibet, had seen a Yeti years ago in the mountains. It had climbed on top of his hut one night and had stayed there until driven off by the old man's yak dung fire. Tenzing also told the group about a wealthy Texan named Tom Slick who wanted to mount a full-scale expedition to track and capture a Yeti.

A twenty-four-year-old Irishman named Peter Byrne felt goosebumps of excitement as Tenzing Norgay told his Yeti stories and mentioned a man who not only shared the dream of discovering the elusive creature, but also had the financial means to do it. Leaving camp the very next day, Byrne trekked down to Sikkim, retrieved Tom Slick's address from Tenzing's wife, and immediately wrote to offer the oilman his services. He stressed the fact that he already had the necessary permits from the Nepalese government and that he spoke the language. Slick's reply did not arrive for several months; for he had spent the winter and early spring in India, just a few hundred miles away from an anxious Peter Byrne, who was ready to switch from guiding tiger hunts for wealthy travelers to searching for the Yeti in his favorite part of the world, the high Himalayas.

June 22, 1956
Dear Peter,
I received your letter and was very interested in it. I am
intrigued with the idea of making another expedition – a
really active one this time – to try to capture a specimen of
the Yeti. I agree with you that your permission to go into
that area is an important element; also your knowledge of
the language would be very helpful. In regard to the permis-
sion, my thought is that we should make it a joint expedi-
tion with the Sherpas and the Nepalese so that they would
get part of the credit if anything was accomplished.

Tom Slick went on to share his past of research on the Yeti and
thoughts about where it might be most likely to live, suggested other
possible members for the expedition, and outlined his plans for financing the adventure.

He reminded the young adventurer that three major discoveries of
the twentieth century had convinced some biologists and zoologists that
there were "fantastic creatures" still to be found. In 1903, the mountain gorilla was seen for the first time in the mountain ranges of
Central Africa; the okapi, a short-necked African animal that looks
something like a donkey-zebra hybrid was found soon after; and in
1938, just as Slick was graduating from Yale with honors, South African fishermen caught a coelacanth in their nets. This last discovery
had been called the most significant zoological find of the twentieth
century since its origins predated the dinosaurs and it was thought
to have vanished into extinction nearly sixty million years ago.

Slick had read articles by popular scientist writers like Willy Ley,
William Winwood Reade, and Philip Henry Gosse, whose stories
about lake monsters, giant squid, and huge sea serpents fueled his
curiosity. When Belgian biologist Bernard Heuvelmans named a new
area of research "cryptozoology" and described it as "the science of
hidden animals," Slick was convinced. He agreed with Heuvelmans
that "hidden" was preferable to "unknown" since such animals are
typically known to local populations, well-described in their story-
telling traditions and oral histories.

The stories of "snowmen" in the Himalayas had fascinated him as a boy; and more current reports had excited him so much that he was planning to mount an expedition. When Byrne contacted him, Slick was ready.

He asked Byrne to contact Cathy McLean, a girlfriend who was living in India, explaining that she knew the expedition plans and Slick's unique personality, and would be able to assess whether Byrne would fit in with the expedition team.

Cathy had known Slick for about a year; they had met the spring before in Palm Beach, at a houseparty revolving around golf and girls. Her beauty and intellect attracted the recently divorced Slick, but her surprise announcement that she was moving to India the following week absolutely captivated him. Soon after the oilman returned to Texas, letters began to arrive from Cathy, from Bombay, New Delhi, and Calcutta, describing the people, parties, and mysterious phenomena that she encountered.

By the fall, she had met the Maharaja of Baroda, through Piloo Modi, a friend and member of the Indian government ministry. Her petite build and pale, almost translucent skin were completely foreign and very alluring; the Maharaja brought Cathy to his palace like a delicate treasure, a porcelain doll he had discovered, a special jewel. During all the years that Cathy lived in India, she always was welcome in Baroda; it was her second home. And what a home it was – an architectural treasure with intricately carved walls and delicately mirrored ceilings, surrounded by lush gardens that smelled of gardenias and other more exotic, unknown scents, and fountains that bubbled with memories of India's majestic past.

When Tom Slick visited India in the spring of 1956, she took him to Baroda, where the Maharaja and his wife welcomed them, offering them a new European influence that included the conveniences of telephones and champagne combined with the regal tradition that Indian royalty had celebrated for centuries. The results were unforgettable – elephant rides, a tiger hunt under a full moon, stories of mysterious *yeh-tehs* in the mountains to the north, and amazing demonstrations by swamis who could walk on hot coals without burning their feet.

Who could resist the magic? Certainly not Tom Slick, whose journeys to India's frontiers of mystery had just begun. His "snow-man hunt" planned for the next winter would be just the beginning of a five year adventure to unknown realms … primitive Nepalese caves, said to be homes of the yeti … the *Brighu Samita*, a magical book written in ancient Sanskrit, purported to hold answers to life's great mysteries … personal audiences with the Dalai Lama, the holy keeper of the Buddhist religion. Like so many pilgrims before him, Tom Slick was searching for his own "holy grail" of sorts; India and its neighboring kingdoms seemed a likely place to find it.

> *June 25, 1956*
> *Dear Maharaja and Princess Usha,*
> *Please forgive me for being so long delayed in writing to thank you for the wonderful hospitality that you showed me on my trip to India in February. The visit with you, complete with tiger hunt and stories of the Yeti, was literally the "high point" of my whole trip.*
> *The two of you could not have been any nicer to Cathy and myself and we had an absolutely marvelous time with you. I will never forget it … it will lead me to the Himalayas next year.*

Cathy McLean and Peter Byrne met in New Delhi, during the summer of 1956. She learned that he had been in the RAF until 1947, and had joined a British tea company with estates in Northern Bengal after the war. He also guided professional tiger hunts along the border of Nepal to offset the boredom of planting tea.

He told Cathy he'd recently driven to Sikkim in his ancient Austin Seven, and trekked with two Sherpas from Gangtok towards Zemu Glacier, where N.A. Tambazi, a Royal Geographic Fellow, had reported a Yeti sighting more than twenty years ago. After finding a single footprint, in the hard snow of a frozen pool near the glaciers, Byrne's Sherpas were anxious to leave the area, sure that a shookpa, another Nepalese word for a Yeti, was nearby. He described their departure, laughing. "We completed the last lap of the trek, some twenty-six miles from Sandakphu to Darjeeling, from ten thousand feet down to two thousand feet and up again to eight thousand feet in one long day." It was obvious that Peter Byrne was fit enough for the strenuous mountain trek; and that he was as intrigued by the Yeti as Tom Slick was. Cathy sent her "approval" of the new expedition member to Texas.

"Peter Byrne was as cool as James Bond," Chuck Slick remembers nearly fifty years later. "When we were kids, he was a big game hunter who knew how to survive in a cave in Nepal, not the usual boring grown-up friend that most parents have."

In the spring of 1957, Peter Byrne joined Tom Slick in New Delhi and they flew together to Kathmandu, where they gathered supplies and porters. Accompanied by Mr. N.D. Bachkheti, an Indian zoologist, and a liaison officer from Nepal, the small group began their reconnaisance expedition, designed to determine whether Slick should fund a much bigger expedition the following year.

Vehicles were scarce in Nepal in 1957, and the best transportation the group of explorers could find was an ancient bus with brakes that did not always work. They traveled southeast, and stopped in a village that was used mostly as a Gerka recruiting post. As the men began to step out of the brightly colored bus, the brakes released and it began to roll, tossing Tom Slick and several others to the rough pavement. It gained speed and the others jumped off frantically; finally it crashed into a big wooden house at the bottom of the hill. Fortunately no one inside was hurt; and the expedition team members suffered only cuts and bruises.

Most of Slick's injuries were to his shins; and the long days of hiking ahead would be particularly painful for him. At the time, he thought only of the mission, never considering that he would not continue. It was only after he returned from Nepal, and told the story of the bus accident, that he admitted how difficult the going had been.

When the team reached the lower mountain ranges bordering the Arun Valley, both Slick and Byrne found clues that each would forever cherish. Byrne found a set of large footprints in soft ground in the *Chhoyang Khola*, at an altitude of about eight thousand feet.

He describes them as "ten inches in length, five-toed prints of a bipedal creature of considerable weight. They were identical to those I'd found in Sikkim years earlier. I'll never forget the eerie thrill of knowing that a Yeti could be just over the next ridge."

In another location nearby, at about ten thousand feet, Slick found similar prints in snow, approximately thirteen inches long. The men photographed their treasures, and made copies using plaster molds. They hurried back to Kathmandu, convinced that a full-scale expedition next year would be worthwhile. Tom Slick couldn't wait to get back to Texas to start planning an all-out effort to capture the Snowman.

From his office in San Antonio he began to pursue a variety of ideas; and his daily correspondence is full of letters inquiring about articles he had read and stories he had heard that somehow made his mind leap forward in its quest to find the Yeti.

In a letter to Mr. Russell Cone, in Los Gatos, California, he explored the possibility of using dogs to track it:

> *Dear Mr. Cone,*
> *I have just read a newspaper article on your hunting dogs making a search for a missing boy in Oregon. I am planning a trip to India and Nepal to search for the "abominable snowman" sometime early next year. I am wondering whether you would have any trained dogs who could hunt these animals. These dogs would be used to try to locate and capture these snowmen in the lower bamboo-forested canyons in the area of Kathmandu (north of), which would be at high alititudes. I would appreciate hearing from you at your earliest convenience.*
> *Thanking you in advance, Tom Slick*

Mr. Cone did not respond to what much have seemed like a very odd letter; but Tom Slick was not deterred. Through family friends in Winston-Salem, North Carolina, he located another source for tracking dogs. He wrote to Mr. E.T. Tillman in Elba, Alabama, and arranged to buy "two or three of the 'man dogs' at two hundred dollars each"; and he asked his secretary to find the best way to ship bloodhounds to Nepal.

More than forty years later, stories of the strange dogs brought to the Arun Valley by the Slick Expedition still are told with excitement in remote villages by the porters who are now old men. They imitate the unique howls with eerie precision, and laugh with delight at the memory of the small "snow boots" that the dogs wore during the trek.

Slick contacted the director of wildlife management at Cornell University, the American Museum of Natural History in New York, and the Georgia State Game Commission in Atlanta, asking each organization about a newly invented tranquilizer gun being used to capture animals. He explained to all three:

> *I am planning an expedition into the Himalayas in the very near future to hunt for the Yeti (more popularly known as the Abominable Snowman), and I have been informed that a hypodermic needle of some kind has been used successfully in shooting game and animals.*
>
> *We, of course, do not want to kill this animal but just capture it and would be interested in having any information you are able to give us on this method.*

In early November, Slick contacted Lynn Bollinger at Helio Aircraft Corporation in Norwood, Massachusetts, about using the Helio Courier plane to fly at a low altitude through the forested areas of Nepal. A month later, he had decided that a Storch observation plane, which could be purchased in Germany, was an even better idea.

Kenneth MacLeish, publisher of *Life Magazine*, had met Slick at party in New York and was interested in the "snowman hunt"; they began to discuss sharing the financial support for the expedition and the exclusive adventure stories and photos that would result. By this point, the expedition budget had climbed to thirty thousand dollars. It included a reconnaissance plane, tracking dogs, state-of-the-art tranquilizer guns, white hunters, Nepalese government liaisons, scientists, Sherpas, photographers, porters, and all of the supplies. The adventure was a month away.

By mid-January, Slick faced a difficult decision. Despite months of trying to line up a co-sponsor to help fund the Yeti expedition, none of his prospects had come through. *Life Magazine* had agreed to send its photographer and some fancy new cameras and film, but he realized that the final bill for the four-month trek in the Himalayas would be his alone.

He thought about his father – the first Tom Slick – *before* he became known as the "king of the wildcatters" with his discoveries of some of the largest oilfields in Oklahoma and Texas. Most people had forgotten his father's first nickname – "Dry Hole Tom" – earned during his earlier oil explorations that were not successful. His namesake chuckled and remembered his father's commitment to risk-taking.

"You'll never succeed unless you try," the older Slick had told his son in 1923, as the two sat together on a riverbank in the woods of western Pennsylvania, weighing the pro's and con's of trying to cross what seemed like a raging torrent to a child, using a fallen tree trunk as a bridge.

"Regrets are mostly for the things we wished we'd tried," the oilman told his son. Young Tom had crawled along the tree trunk and crossed the river in 1923; he decided to fund the entire Yeti expedition and went home to pack for Nepal.

At the very last moment, just weeks before the expedition team's departure, an unexpected co-sponsor decided to put up half the financing for the adventure. During a rather ordinary oil business meeting in Ft. Worth, a wildcatter named Kirk Johnson was fascinated when Slick described the upcoming expedition that he decided to fund half of it. Later, Johnson would explain that Slick's enthusiasm and certainty about the Yeti were incredibly powerful; he "just couldn't resist."

In early 1958 the *Slick-Johnson Snowman Expedition*, got underway. A highly respected American naturalist named Gerald Russell was field leader. Inspired by his earlier participation on the *Daily Mail Expedition* in 1955, Russell was convinced the group would find its Yeti in the Himalayas. Professional photographer George Holton and German movie-maker Norman Dyrhenfurth both would document the journey; and Peter Byrne and his brother Bryan would use their superb hunting skills and knowledge of the mountains to track the elusive Yeti. Captain Pushkar Shumsher Jung Bahadur Rana was appointed by the government of Nepal to accompany the expedition. Ten Sherpa guides and sixty-five porters were also engaged for the expedition; and Byrne set about arranging for food and supplies in Kathmandu.

"Food was difficult," he remembers today. "Most of it was canned stuff from India and we ended up throwing a lot away when we opened it. We learned that it was actually easier to buy fresh food from the villages we passed through; and by the last expedition that's what we did. And of course our bottle of Scotch was important on all the expeditions."

Breakfast usually consisted of eggs, tea or coffee, and a *chapatti*, the Nepalese version of a tortilla, made from a coarse flour called *ata*. The team members did not stop for lunch, but sometimes snacked on another *chapatti*. Dinner around the campfire might include rice (at the lower altitudes) or potatoes (at the higher altitudes), perhaps roasted chicken or goat, and *dal*, a hearty lentil soup that is a staple in the mountains. Conversation always turned to the group's mysterious quarry; Sherpas shared the legends they'd heard from their grandparents about the *meh-teh* ("manlike thing that is not a man") or the *dzu-teh* ("big thing"); after a few sips of Scotch, the explorers would go to their tents to dream of a capture just beyond the next mountain or valley.

From base camps that were established in the upper Arun Valley, search parties fanned out to interview Sherpa villagers and search for evidence of the Yeti. Whenever a Sherpa passed along a story about a possible sighting, it took days and sometimes a week to reach that location. And in keeping with Tenzing Norgay's earlier warning, the cunning creature had always moved on. After three months, a Sherpa named Da Temba announced he had seen a Yeti, but Gerald Russell, who was a part of the small search party, did not see it.

From its grand beginnings and large entourage of explorers and would-be explorers, the expedition dwindled as the forays from mountain forests to higher peaks became more challenging and temperatures dropped; and after four months only Byrne, his brother Bryan, and a few Sherpas remained in the game. After another five months, the last yeti hunters trekked slowly back to Kathmandu, using the last of their stores, disappointed that the last nine months had not produced more evidence.

The next year, only Peter and Bryan Byrne returned to the mountains, retained by Tom Slick at the salary of just one hundred dollars per month, but driven by something far more compelling than financial reward. They took no tents and no food, planning to live off the land and sleep like the native shepherds do, in caves and wood shelters.

Traveling so lightly meant the Yeti hunters could move quickly, like the elusive creature himself; and the Byrne brothers covered huge amounts of Nepalese ground during the next nine months. At *Pangboche* temple, the lamas claimed to have a sacred Yeti scalp, which looked convincing to the Byrnes, and may still be protected there. Another famous – or infamous – scalp was brought back from Nepal by Sir Edmund Hillary in 1960; it was proven to be a fake, made from the skin of a Serow, a goat antelope. Byrne is convinced that the fake scalp was made by a Tibetan taxidermist years before to help ease the inter-temple rivalry that existed between the numerous temples and monasteries of Pangboche, Thyangboche and Kumjung; Hillary believes he retrieved the original scalp, not a copy, and that it was indeed a fake.

While the Slick team chose to leave the sacred scalp in the *Pangboche* Temple, they could not resist stealing one finger of the sacred Yeti hand that also was displayed there. Legends of the hand had traveled as far as London, and during an expedition-planning session with biologists in England in 1958, Dr. Osman Hill had encouraged Tom Slick and his team to bring back the thumb for study. To help, Dr. Hill presented them with a human hand, removed from an English cadaver in his laboratory, suggesting they switch the human thumb with the thumb on the sacred Yeti hand.

"I'll never forget looking into the brown paper bag that Osmond Hill brought with him to lunch at Claridge's," Peter Byrne says with a laugh, more than forty years later. I also had to be rather creative when I traveled with the thumb to Nepal; I carried it in an empty film cannister."

When he got back to *Pangboche* Temple, Byrne performed the tricky operation with the consent of the head lama, with the dim glow of butter lamps as his only light. He switched the thumbs because only that digit would establish the link between the creature and *homo sapiens*. But Byrne was more fascinated by the index finger of the Yeti hand. "It was a longer finger and had a very long dark fingernail on it," he remembers, wondering about its significance. "It may still be in Pangboche," he adds.

After switching the thumbs, Byrne went to Calcutta, where he joined actor Jimmy Stewart and his wife, Gloria, for dinner at the Grand Hotel. His description of his adventures at *Pangboche* Temple enthralled the Stewarts, and they were curious about the scientific ramifications that would result from study of the "Yeti thumb". They agreed to smuggle the stolen appendage into England, and handed it over to Osman Hill. Tests supposedly were conducted; and Hill's early results described in letters to Slick appeared promising, but vague. No scientific data were published; and the ill-gotten "Yeti thumb" disappeared after Hill's death a few years later. Some cryptozoologists like Dr. Richard Greenwell still hope the mysterious digit will be re-discovered and subjected to modern DNA technology, which would provide some definitive answers.

Peter Byrne spent his last winter in Nepal with his brother, in a cave in the upper *Chhoyang Khola*, one of the deep gorges that runs into the headwaters of the Arun river in the northeastern part of the tiny mountain kingdom, not far from where he had found a footprint three years before. Exhausted and low on food and supplies, the men had encountered deep winter snows and temperatures as low as 45 degrees below zero. One evening, as they sat around their fire inside the cave, a Sherpa runner arrived with a letter from Tom Slick.

Still fit and handsome at seventy-five years old, Peter Byrne smiles at the memory of two young adventurers in a cave in the middle of Nepal, greeting a man who had just run 140 miles in four days to bring them instructions. The three-year hunt for the Snowman in the Himalayas was over. Now Tom Slick had a new quarry in site, closer to home; and he wanted Peter and Bryan Byrne to join him in a new search for Bigfoot in the Pacific Northwest.

Science Hunts 'Snowman'

By TOM SLICK
(Copyright 1958)

I believe in the existence of the Abominable Snowman—the so-called "legend" of the high slopes of the Himalayas.

Recently I told this to a doubting friend. When he scoffed at my belief, I told him that I thought the Yeti—as the Sherpas call the Snowman—would be found before the end of 1958. And that the creature would prove to be higher up the evolutionary scale than the ape. And, further, that if I were proved wrong I would donate a thousand dollars to his favorite charity.

Before any mistaken conclusions are drawn, let me emphasize that this does not signify that I take the

LEADER—Tom Slick of San Antonio is official leader and co-sponsor (with Kirk Johnson of Fort Worth) of search for the Yeti.

matter lightly. Far from it, Indeed, it indicates how nearly positive I am in my own mind that the Yeti exists as a humanoid creature. The search for it is surely a scientific project of major importance which could add immeasurably to our knowledge of mankind.

Indeed, I have myself made journeys to the Himalayan area. Last year, I sponsored and led an expedition there in search of the Yeti. And, at this moment, the Slick-Johnson Nepal Snowman Expedition is trekking into the largely unexplored, uninhabited Upper Arun River region of the high Himalayas on a new quest, using fresh and exciting methods, equipment and ideas that sprang largely from last year's unsuccessful attempt to present a Yeti to a still-doubting world.

I believe that today, next week, or several weeks from now a report may come out of that ancient wilderness telling that an expedition member has at last come face to face with a fierce and hairy ape-man, eight feet tall.

My interest in the Yeti was first aroused a few years ago when, on a visit to India, I heard vague reports of an ape-man creature roaming the snowy slopes of Nepal, Tibet and the surrounding highlands. In 1954, when a British expedition spent months in a vain, but in some ways encouraging, search for the creature my interest deepened.

Then, in 1956, I made a reconnaissance of my own into the fringes of the high Himalayas. I talked to caravan people coming out of the mountains and to other natives who claimed to have glimpsed the Yeti. Still doubting, I asked these people to describe the creatures.

AT ABOUT this same time Peter Byrne, an Irish journalist and hunter-explorer, was making a reconnaissance of his own in the Sikkim area of Nepal. We met and exchanged accounts of our investigations. Byrne, who speaks Nepalese, had kept verbatim records of his talks with natives. From his notebook, he read me the following question and answer sequence:

ROUTE—Map shows where expedition will center its search in Asian mountains.

Q. "What do you think it is—a man or an animal?"
A. "It is a hairy man. It walks on two feet as a man does."
Q. "What does it eat?"
A. "The same as the yaks (wild oxen)—trees, grass, bushes."
Q. "What does it look like?"
A. "Like a big man, with hair all over. The hair is red, but we believe it changes color in winter. It has a pointed head."
"Q. Does it kill animals or man?"
A. "Yes. A man was killed in a village near Punakha last monsoon time. The Yeti broke his neck and tore his clothes off. His relatives found him, with tracks of the Yeti in the earth all around the body."

These answers tallied closely to those I had gathered in my own interrogations. Further, the men I questioned said the creatures were not bears or apes, which they would recognize, but walked erect and had no tails. These descriptions contradicted the theories of some western scientists who have been trying for years to explain the Yeti "legend" in terms of mistaken identity. The creature,

HE'S A BIG BOY—Artist's conception of the giant Yeti dwarfs man. Descriptions put him at eight feet tall. Some reports say Yeti has killed Sherpas without provocation.

say these conservative scientists, is probably a snow leopard. Or a langur monkey. Or a Himalayan red bear.

HOWEVER, in recent years strange footprints have been found and photographed just above the snowline of Nepal. These footprints up to thirteen inches long and nearly half that wide, with no indentation of a human arch but more closely resembling the track of man than any animal.

Neither the tracks of the snow leopard, the langur monkey, nor the red bear fit that description. And the bare footprints of man himself are different in shape, shorter and less chunky.

By the time I was ready to return home to San Antonio I had become convinced that the existence of the Yeti as a missing link between ape and man was a scientific long shot worth real investigation. Besides, the mystery challenged my love of adventure. At its lowest level, this would be a chance to hunt a rare and probably dangerous animal — perhaps the most dangerous animal alive.

I made up my mind to finance and lead an expedition for the following year on a quest for the Yeti. Peter Byrne agreed to join me.

In that we did not actually see, photograph or capture a Yeti, the results of that expedition were negative. But we did find and photograph Yeti footprints. We did follow three sets of the creature's tracks until we lost them on

rocky terrain or had to give up due to failing light. And we did collect 15 eyewitness accounts of sightings.

Further than all that, by showing photographs of apes, monkeys, bears and an artist's drawing of a prehistoric ape-man to these eyewitnesses, we asked them to choose the ones that most nearly resembled the Yeti. The unanimity of choice was impressive. Details of these findings will be related in a later article.

Last year, also, the first Russian expedition to the Pamir Mountains, on the far side of the Himalayas, reported sighting a Yeti. Soviet scientists A.C. Promin, of the University of Leningrad, said he watched the creature for five minutes and that it was "stocky, having long arms and a body covered with grayish-brown hair."

BUT APPARENTLY the Yeti is as controversial a creature in Russia as it is in the West. In February, a group of Promin's colleagues wrote a letter to Izvestia declaring they did not believe his claim of a sighting.

My own belief, however, has strengthened with each new scrap of evidence. Now I am almost sure that the creature does exist as an as-yet undiscovered anthropoid type. All that remains to make that belief 100 per cent is the photographed proof of a sighting or the actual capture of a Yeti. If such proof comes this year the whole world will be the richer for it.

Article by Tom Slick, published in the *San Antonio Express* in 1958 (copyright Tom Slick), describing his first yeti expedition and his reasons for believing in the "snowman". (*Tom Slick Letters/Photo Collection.*)

Slick's trips to India, Nepal and Tibet in the mid-1950s were full of the mystery and rich cultural experiences that those countries offer. From snake charmers in Delhi to moon-lit elephant rides in Baroda, from weekends in a maharaja's palace to an audience at the Dalai Lama's summer retreat in Tibet, Slick's journeys were filled with excitement. (*Photos courtesy of the Mind Science Foundation.*)

OILMAN TOM SLICK (C) AND PARTNERS JOIN SNOWMAN SEARCH
F. Kirk Johnson jr. (L) and W. E. Randall to field expeditions.

2 Expeditions

Lure of Snowman

Oilman Tom Slick, Saturday reported he and partners are fielding two more expeditions in search of the abominable snowman.

One of the groups is already deep in the Himalayas, sending out occasional messages by runner.

JUNGLE TRIP

Another will push into the Sumatran jungle.

Slick's Nepal expedition into the Himalayas a l s o will be sponsored by F. Kirk Johnson, president of Ambassador Oil corp., and the San Antonio Zoological society.

Johnson will join Slick in the Sumatra expedition, which will be sponsored and led by Trapper Peter Rhyiner.

Rhyiner, whom Slick called a world famous trapper, recently uncovered tracks while on another Sumatran expedition. There is reason to believe, S l i c k said, that the tracks were made by an Orang-Pendek.

The O r a n g-Pendek, Slick said, is believed to be similar to the abominable snowman, known also as the Yeti.

Slick said he believes there are three types of snowmen—small, medium-sized and large. The small would be four feet tall, the medium five or six feet and the large about eight feet.

MEDIUM SIZE

He thinks the Orang-Pendek corresponds to the medium snowman.

Snowmen-type creatures or their t r a c k s have been reported in North and S o u t h American a n d Africa, Slick said. He thinks they may exist any place into which man has not yet penetrated deeply.

Slick said he is confident the expeditions will bring back new evidence of the s n o w-man's existence, if not the snowman himself. Slick lost a $1000 bet to Otto A. Koehler, Pearl brewery president, that he would capture or photograph a snowman during 1958. Koehler gave the money to Trinity university. C. W. Walker, board chairman, accepted it.

Slick reported the Soviet Union also is interested in the snowman.

RUSSIAN CONFAB

It is now fielding three expeditions, and one announced recently to Nepal may be a fourth, Slick said. He said he went to Russia in September, to talk things over with Russian scientists and received a cordial reception.

He said he will co-operate fully with Russia's expedition, with both groups interested in scientific research.

He said if a snowman is found, it would be one of the greatest scientific discoveries in the history of t' e world.

The Nepal expedition is led by Peter Byrne, an Irishman from Australia who in the past has been, among other things, a journalist. It has more than 30 men in the party and is "traveling light," Slick said.

JUST RETURNED

F. Kirk Johnson jr., son of one of the sponsors, just returned from a Nepal expedition and probably will go again. He and William Randall, representative of Johnson sr., joined Slick for his announcement meeting in San Antonio.

Slick himself will not join his expedition unless a snowman is captured.

However, he said, he remains the expeditions' official leader.

The Slick-Johnson Expedition was the largest "yeti hunt" of the 1950s, led by explorer Peter Byrne, with a team of experts ranging from a zoologist to world-famous photographer Norman Dyhrenfurth. (*Article courtesy of the* San Antonio Express *Collection.*)

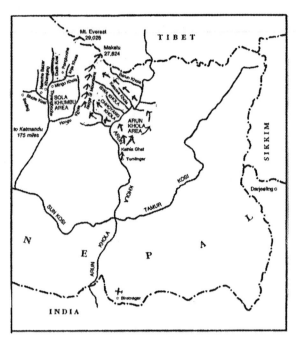

Expeditions in 1957, 1959, and 1959 explored the remote Arun Khola and Chhoyang Khola areas of Eastern Nepal, steadily climbing towards Mt. Makalu, the world's fifth highest mountain. (*Map courtesy of Tom Slick Collection.*)

Yeti Expedition, Nepal, 1957. Back row, left to right, Tom Slick, Peter Byrne; front row, Nepali team. (*Peter Byrne Photo Collection.*)

Yeti Expedition, 1957. Nepali porters cross the Sun Kosi River in a dugout canoe. (*Peter Byrne Photo Collection.*)

Yeti Expedition 1957. Dense jungle, leeches, and heavy rain intensified the challenges of the trek. (*Peter Byrne Photo Collection.*)

Although the elusive yeti was Slick's quarry, he was fascinated by evidence of "mind-over-matter" phenomena in the Himalayas; and his diaries contain insights he obtained from monks he met along the journey. (*Photo courtesy of the Mind Science Foundation.*)

Peter Byrne is given a "yeti scalp" by the head lama at Pengboche Monastery. (*Peter Byrne Photo Collection.*)

1958 Yeti Expedition Team with tracking dogs. Left to right, Bryan Byrne (Dublin, Ireland), Nepalese Liaison Officer Pushkar Shumsher, Gerald Russell (explorer who brought the first Pandas to New York in the 1920s), Peter Byrne, expedition leader, and expedition photographer Norman Dyrhenfurth. (*Peter Byrne Photo Collection.*)

Peter and Bryan Byrne test the newest animal dart-guns during the 1958 Yeti Expediton. (*Photo by George Holton; Peter Byrne Photo Collection.*)

The Slick-Johnson Snowman Expedition, 1959. (*Peter Byrne Photo Collection.*)

The Slick-Johnson Snowman Expedition, 1959. (*Peter Byrne Photo Collection.*)

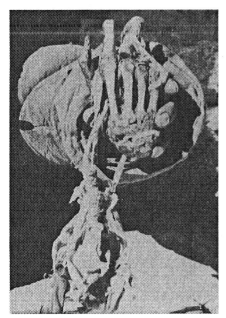
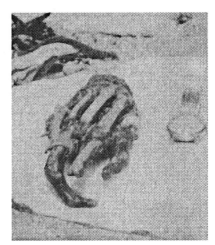

With the head lama's consent, expedition leader Peter Byrne removed the thumb of this yeti hand on display in the Pangboche Monastery, for scientific study. More than forty years later, he wonders about the significance of the dark, longer fingernail on the middle finger. (*Photos by Peter Byrne.*)

Yeti footprints, 1959 Yeti Expedition. (*Photo by Peter Byrne.*)

Chapter Eight
An Open Door Policy
(1955 – 1960)

Between the appetizer course and a feast of roasted pheasant, guests at Tom Slick's dinner party discussed the long table's unusual centerpiece – a large plaster casting of a Yeti footprint.

"A mind scientist, a financier, a big game hunter and a beautiful babe were all there," Slick's brother Earl remembers. "It was a typical gathering at Tom's – diverse friends and something interesting to talk about. There was a lively discussion about whether the footprint was real; and bets were made that a Yeti would finally be captured as the decade of the 1960s began."

A waterfall cascaded down one wall of the dining room, and paintings by Picasso, O'Keefe, Braque and a chimpanzee named Betty dominated the walls. Built by renowned Texas architect O'Neil Ford, whose award-winning designs included Trinity University in Texas, Skidmore College in New York City, and the famous Santa Maria Beach Club in Lima, Peru, the house was a showcase of contemporary style. A sprawling one-story building, with low ceilings and Frank Lloyd Wright-inspired windows, it was surrounded by two acres of lush gardens with a beautiful dark rock swimming pool, in the heart of the city's most affluent neighborhood, just a few blocks from the Urschel mansion where his mother and stepfather lived.

Slick and Ford worked well together on the design and building phases of the project, perhaps because the architect genuinely enjoyed his client's constant questions, ideas, and suggestions. In a rather daring move, they decided to utilize the "Lift-Slab" method of construction developed at Southwest Research Institute in collaboration with Phillip Youtz in 1951. It was an innovative technique used mainly for multi-story buildings, where concrete slabs are poured at ground level, one on top of the other, and then lifted into place on top of columns using hydraulic jacks. There were obvious economic advantages to this method since it used a minimal amount of formwork and allowed year-round construction. It also developed an excellent safety record since much of the work was done on the ground, minimizing the chances of a workman falling.

There were a few instances of failure, however. During construction of Serra High School in San Mateo, California, in 1954, a slab fell due to column instability; and in 1962 a similar accident occurred in Marion, Indiana, when a portion of the roof slab of the Girls Dormitory at Marion College collapsed during construction.

Confident that the new construction method was sound and destined for an important future, Slick and Ford wanted to demonstrate the technique in San Antonio. On May 4, 1958, just a few days before Slick's Birthday, he and Bill Rhame hosted a Lift Slab Party at his new home site at 400 Devine Road.

Friends stood on the slab, which also had an open bar, musicians, and a photographer, as it was lifted to roof level; some guests still remember the slow but exciting ride. Rhame recalled that "the only drawback was having to climb down a ladder to get to the 'powder room.'"

Adjoining the house, the garages held Slick's own collection of cars that included an elegant green Cadillac and the ultra-sporty car of the times, a Lincoln Continental, with cream-colored interior leather. A motorized miniature Model-T also was parked in the garage, the prized possession of his sons, nine-year-old Tom and seven-year-old Charles.

Always appreciative of beauty and exotic touches, Slick filled the house with art, music, family and friends. Just off the master bedroom, a deep Japanese bathtub opened out to a small private garden with bonsai trees and polished stones. Augusto, the houseman, kept hot sake near the tub, as well as thick terrycloth robes. The ambiance reminded Slick of his adventures in the Orient, a world away from San Antonio. Twenty years later, hot tubs would become the rage in the United States; and everyone lucky enough to have seen or sampled Tom Slick's spectacular bathroom would realize they had enjoyed a glimpse into the future.

Although his two marriages had ended in divorce, Slick remained good friends with both ex-wives and a very involved father with his four children. When he built his remarkable bachelor's home in 1958, its creative nooks and crannies and spirit of fun made it "the place to be". Beautiful women longed to be invited to visit; and Slick's children and their friends were equally as enthralled.

Patty Slick was ten years old when her father's house was completed. She walked into her newly decorated room, discovering lush silks in shades of purple, blue and green; and her own sunken tub in the bathroom. Her father told her that she would visit other countries someday, experience other cultures, and realize that beauty was vastly diverse.

The fabulous silks in Patty's room had come from Bangkok, Thailand, ordered from the famous Jim Thompson, who would disappear very mysteriously a few years later. Slick had been entertained by the designer during his trip around the world in 1956, and was very impressed by the burgeoning silk company that Thompson had built, using the talented weavers from the Thai jungle. Many years later, rumors that both Slick and Thompson were gathering intelligence information about Communist activities in that part of the world for the OSS (the predecessor of the CIA) would surface. Thompson's sudden disappearance from Thailand and his booming export business never was solved.

"One of the very nicest experiences of my trip was to have dinner in your attractive home," Slick wrote to Thompson. He continued with compliments about the new Thai Silk Company, noting, "You should be very proud of your creativity in producing such beautiful, unique material," and requested that Thompson send him more. He ordered silk table cloths and napkins, one set in "fairly small checks – probably grey or brown or black" for his own long dining table, and one set for his mother "in a light pink and pastel mixture."

In touch with his feminine side, long before bestselling books began to instruct men how to discover that wholeness, Slick enjoyed selecting lovely accessories for his family and friends; and he often personally directed the details, including what color they should be.

For his daughter's eleventh birthday, he organized "Patty's Pink Pajama Party", directing his secretary/assistant Jeri Walsh to make *everything* pink – from the invitations to the party favors, to all the food the little girls ate.

He put the same thoughtfulness into the gifts he ordered and the evenings he planned for his numerous girlfriends. Slick's women friends were all beautiful and intelligent, sprinkled over the globe, from Beverly Hills to Beirut, from New York to New Delhi.

"Wear flat shoes," Josephine Gill advised her statuesque friend, Nancy de Herrera. "Tom doesn't like women who are taller than he is." Josephine had known Slick for many years; her husband was his hunting buddy; and the families had shared weekend house parties on neighboring Texas ranches and many fascinating meals together at "the most interesting dining room table in town."

Nancy de Herrera was a beautiful blonde young widow from California, who was spending the first half of 1960 in New York, learning more about the fashion industry in preparation for her new job as an "Ambassadress of Fashion" for newspaper columnist Cobina Wright. Still grieving over the death of her husband, an astonishingly handsome man from Argentina who had played polo, raced cars, was the country's amateur golf champion *and* a wonderful husband, Nancy would be hard to please in matchmaking attempts. Near look-alikes, Nancy and Josephine had been friends for years; and now that Nancy was recently widowed, an introduction to Tom Slick was inevitable.

"The first thing I noticed about Tom was those silver-blue eyes," de Herrera recalled more than forty years later. "We were relaxed, warm friends right away. He talked a lot, like an encyclopedia, but not about personal things.

"Dating Tom was far from ordinary. He would telephone from Timbuktu to ask me to dinner the following week; the idea of being pursued from some remote corner of the world was quite exciting," she added with smile. Other women friends report similar calls and letters; the technique certainly produced far more anticipation and acceptances than the usual single businessman telephoning from his office downtown.

Something unusual was always a part of time spent with Slick. Before a romantic dinner at an elegant restaurant, he took one date to a quick pre-dinner appointment with a struggling inventor, working in his garage to invent a seamless tin can. Slick was intrigued; the woman was more skeptical.

Family, friends, and people who met Tom Slick only briefly all were struck by his immense curiosity about everything, and his willingness to investigate and explore. As a result of his ready-to-try-anything personality, his life was interesting and filled with fun. His children remember him "always smiling"; business partners describe him as an optimist who always looked ahead and did not dwell on past disappointments.

Some of his best friends recall that he was gullible at times. Dr. Robert V. West, Jr., who ran the Slick Oil Company, found himself wanting to protect his boss from the constant flow of would-be investment seekers; attorney Jesse Oppenheimer was inspired by Slick's creativity in structuring new deals, but worried that some of the people who pitched the deals were taking advantage of "a man whose door was always open."

But think about the opposite of "gullible" for a moment. A very creative thinker, former CEO of the *International Herald Tribune* and previous president of the Rockefeller Foundation, Peter Goldmark, suggests that "numb" might be a good antonym. "The numb hand cannot feel warmth or cold. The numb heart cannot experience joy or sorrow. The numb mind cannot imagine the possibilities of life that are occurring all around us, all the time."

Tom Slick was never numb. Whether he was pursuing the Yeti, or a cure for cancer, or a new oil recovery technology, or a new world order that focused on peace, or the best food in town, he was passionately awake and present, never numb.

"We were eating an extraordinary meal at Antoine's in New Orleans, with all the elaborate sauces, many courses, and fine wines that have made that restaurant famous," Bob West remembered. The two men were in Louisiana to investigate a new secondary oil recovery process that Slick hoped West would use in the oil company.

Conversation shifted from the oil business to childhood memories. "Tom did not often talk about the past," West said, "but the topic of the Great Depression came up, and the difficulties that most families experienced in 1929, 1930, and 1931.

"Of course the Slick family had tremendous, unbelievable wealth, at a time when not many people did. Tom was preparing to go to Exeter Academy, and his mother wanted him outfitted properly. She sent the chauffeur to downtown Oklahoma City, with four-teen-year-old Tom in the backseat, instructing him to buy several pairs of new shoes for the year away at school.

"After picking two or three pairs of shoes, Tom heard a mother and father with a younger boy discover that they could not afford the pair of shoes their son had selected. Quietly he asked the chauffeur, who was preparing to pay for Tom's shoes, to put back a pair and anonymously pay for the other boy's shoes."

Seventy years later, tears fill Bob West's eyes. "It was such a glimpse of the man," he explains. "His generosity, without any expectation of recognition for it, always touched me deeply."

Apparently it touched legions. When Slick died in 1962, letters arrived from all over the world; each writer felt that he or she had lost a best friend; each shared a story of some kindness on Slick's part – encouragement, a job, a loan, a special experience.

Tom Slick often talked about the importance of his interesting and diverse friends, calling them a "major source of happiness, along with my family."

In a very special audience with His Holiness, the fourteenth Dalai Lama, in Lhasa in 1957 (just months before the spiritual leader fled to Dharamsala, India, on the eve of Chinese occupation), the subjects of friendship and enlightenment came up. Slick's diary records these words from the Dalai Lama:

"Whenever I meet people I always approach them from the standpoint of basic things we have in common. We each have a physical structure, a mind, emotions. Looking at others from this perspective, rather than emphasizing the differences – such as the fact that I am Tibetan, or a different color, or religion, or cultural background – allows me to have a feeling that I am meeting someone just the same as me."

In a postscript, Slick writes, "I know what he means! When I meet new people, I always approach them from the standpoint of common ground. That way it's always easy to find a connection."

According to Slick's journal, despite the political turmoil of the moment, His Holiness had appeared calm and smiling, as if he had all the time in the world to chat about unexplained phenomena and consciousness.

"You Westerners have the constraints of the idea that everything can be explained within the framework of a single lifetime," he said, almost chuckling. "And you combine it with the notion that everything can and must be explained and accounted for."

Part of Slick's soul resonated to the message that not everything could be explained, at least not in this lifetime. And he knew with certainty that as soon as "answers" did emerge, new questions would replace the old ones.

The mystery-hunting side of Slick could not abandon the quest, nor did the Dalai Lama suggest he should. Instead, he shared his thoughts with this odd pilgrim from Texas and sent him to see his most devout monks. Contemplation and meditation filled the next days in Lhasa; and the powers of mindfulness and intention were clearly and dramatically demonstrated. Slick began to envision his next research institute while still in the mountain sanctuary; he envisioned it built alongside Southwest Foundation and Southwest Research Institute, an important addition to his original concept of a Science City on the Texas range. After all, shouldn't science and spirit work together?

Sharing his lifelong dream to find solutions to life's most complex mysteries, Slick clasped his hands together in the respectful *namaste* greeting and bowed deeply. His Holiness's eyes twinkled with humor. "How long do you have to spend here?" he asked.

"One week," Slick replied; and the Dalai Lama laughed his gentle laugh.

After this remarkable encounter in Lhasa in 1957, which Slick later described as "life altering", he returned to the United States to establish his fifth scientific research institute. He named it the Mind Science Foundation; and by September, 1958, it was chartered as a not-for-profit operating foundation, with the purpose of scientifically studying "the vast potential of the human mind." Dr. Wilford Hahn, a biochemist in Southwest Foundation's first core group of six scientists, was appointed director of the new organization. Slick also invited Dr. Andre Puharich, director of the Round Table Foundation in Glen Cover, Maine, to serve as an adviser on ESP (extra sensory perception) research, and Dr. K.T. Jahagirdar, a professor of Psychology in Bombay, India, to design a study of "mental healing."

Slick asked family members and close friends to serve as the first Trustees. His sister Betty Moorman (who had long ago made her brother promise to investigate the ghostly mysteries of their childhood home) and brother-in-law Lew, his stepbrother Charles Urschel and his wife Betty, his business adviser Bill Rhame, and his attorney Jesse Oppenheimer were the first names on his list. He asked another friend, a Texas/California hybrid, C.V. ("Woody") Wood, Jr., to play an even bigger role.

Woody was a Texan by birth; and he took his cowboy boots and exaggerated twang to California in 1948, where he helped develop Disneyland in the 1950s, ran McCullough Oil Company in the 1960s and 1970s, and worked on movie company mergers for Warner Brothers in the 1980s. As impressive as his professional credentials were, he needed bigger challenges to satisfy an imagination and curiosity that nearly matched Slick's. But when the two first met at a party in the Beverly Hills Hotel, they seemed worlds apart.

Slick was strikingly handsome, intellectual, dressed in a well-tailored suit, quietly studying everyone in the room. Wood was boisterous, gregarious, smoking a cigar, wearing snakeskin boots and a loud sports coat.

Despite very different outward appearances, they recognized exciting common ground – a deep belief in the huge, untapped potential of the human mind and a fascination about strange, unexplained phenomena. A friendship that would last a lifetime was formed; at last Slick had a partner in adventure, with both the curiosity and the financial means to ferret out the mysteries that intrigued him. The unlikely new partners in mystery hunting began to look for unexplained phenomena ... and Woods' adopted home state of California seemed to be full of them.

Old friends describe Woods' bachelor house as "something from a Halloween horror film – garish, fun, and truly amazing in its own way. All the shelves in the bar were filled with those little liquor bottles you pick up on airplanes," and Woody himself as "a wonderful circus barker, always enticing his audience to experience the next magic act."

In the late 1950s Woody married Joanne Dru, a beautiful and sophisticated actress who often co-starred with John Wayne. She smoothed some of her husband's rough edges and built a beautiful new home in the posh Truesdale Estates of Beverly Hills; but despite the elegance, cowboy boots remained on Woody's feet and mystery on his mind.

Slick's children were all pre-teens in the late 1950s, but they remember Woody as "one of the greatest characters" they ever knew. Their friendship with him lasted into adulthood; and long after their father's death in 1962, Woody continued to serve as a Lifetime Trustee of the Mind Science Foundation.

It was C.V. Wood who convinced Israeli psychic Uri Geller to come to the United States to be studied by the Foundation in 1972; and Geller's spoon bending demonstrations on *The Tonight Show with Johnny Carson* a few years later led to tremendous public interest and a multitude of research projects that attempted to document "mind over matter" (psychokinesis), extrasensory perception (ESP), and clairvoyance. Until his death in 1987, Woody continued to contribute funds and advice to the Mind Science Foundation, encouraging its researchers to carry on the mystery hunt that first began at Tom Slick's dinner table. For in addition to making serious intellectual presentations to credible institutions and scientific laboratories, to interest them in "mind science", Slick also had some fun with the burgeoning field of parapsychology by inviting friends to participate in hands-on research.

"We were all at dinner one night," longtime friend Patsy Steves recalls, "when Tom asked everyone for their car keys. He passed them to a psychic named Peter Hurkos, who was visiting from

California and didn't know any of the guests. The psychic told us each something about ourselves; and all of his observations were accurate. It was amazing"

A few years later, the same dinner format was expanded, and the exclusive dining club, The Argyle, became a site for paranormal adventure. Dr. Henry K. Puharich, one of the first scientists with a doctorate in parapsychology, presented ESP (extra sensory perception) experiments, impressing Slick so much that he suggested to his friends at the Worcester Foundation in Shrewsbury, Massachusetts that they consider studying the electric fields that Puharich claimed increased his sensitivity. "What we need is an open-minded scientist to check this field so that some of us visionary people won't fool ourselves too much," Slick said.

The Foos family from Richmond, Virginia, also attended an Argyle evening to demonstrate a remarkable claim – the ability to "see" without the use of their eyes. Slick first met Foos in 1957, during a drip to Washington, DC, where he met with Dr. Harvey Savely, Chairman of the Medical Division of the United States Air Force, to discuss the impact that "mind science" might have on military research.

While Savely could not offer financial support "because of vulnerable political situations", he suggested that Slick meet a man in Virginia who seemed to possess "extra retinal vision" (ERV). Slick decided to investigate; and a few weeks after the meeting, he brought Foos, his daughter and niece to San Antonio.

Finally, Peter Hurkos was invited to repeat his fascinating performance with dinner guests' car keys, and to demonstrate other examples of his psychic abilities.

An invitation from Tom Slick was highly sought after, and the Argyle Club's dinner program quickly sold out. San Antonio's social set, all dressed beautifully for the evening, arrived at the club with their husbands in tow. The men were the city's business elite; they admired Slick's intelligence, civic contributions and wealth; they were curious, but skeptical about his newest research interest.

Slick introduced Puharich, Foos and Hurkos and the show began. Perhaps the most dramatic was the Foos demonstration, described later by Slick:

"Mr. Foos's young daughter was very carefully blindfolded under our supervision so that we can assume she could see nothing; neither was there any possibility of intelligence between any unblindfolded person and the daughter. After this, the girl demonstrated conclusively that she cannot only 'see' but can see in complete detail, including such things as looking up names and numbers in the local telephone book."

The audience was fascinated; and ESP, unexplained sight, and psychic predictions were the topics at dinner parties and golf courses for weeks. But Slick was having trouble convincing the U.S. scientific community to take the field of mind science seriously. Never discouraged, he looked to scientific organizations in Europe.

He wrote to the French National Academy of Science, following up on a lead that a prominent French banker, R. de Lailhacar, had given him at a party after a polo match in Jaipur, India. According to the banker, the French Academy was supporting experiments in the field of levitation, something that had long fascinated Slick, who had seen Buddhist monks demonstrate the feat of "mind over gravity" firsthand in Tibet.

He predicted that soon more and more people would master this ability; and upon returning to the United States, it appeared that his pronouncement had been true. Millions of people had witnessed an ordinary-looking man from California float in mid-air on national television.

Delighted, Slick immediately wrote to Art Baker, the host of the popular show "You Asked for It", requesting the performer's name and address. Today, it's doubtful a network would provide that information; but 1957 was a gentler, more trusting era; and Slick was soon in touch with Mr. Jim Crabe, of Santa Monica, California.

He told Crabe of his interest in levitation and "mind over matter," stressing his desire to study these phenomena scientifically. "We are not asking you to reveal any secrets if there is magic or trickery involved in your act," Slick assured him. "However, if you are performing this feat without mechanical aids and would be willing to give a demonstration in front of a group of scientists, we would be most interested in hearing from you." He thoughtfully assured the levitator that his reply would be completely confidential, with no fear of adverse publicity.

Crabe was an honest man. He replied that he was a magician, which gave Slick an exciting new idea. In all future evening programs to demonstrate the paranormal, he would also invite a magician who would attempt to duplicate the various presentations. This appealed to Slick's curiosity as well as his sense of fairness. The twist was well received; and more than forty-five years later, everyone who attended an early Mind Science Foundation program remembers it vividly. The magician as the scientific "control" in parapsychology experiments continues today, and the Amazing Randi has become an important spokesperson for all skeptical inquirers.

As the decade of the 1960s began, Slick's major interest was in mind science; but his fascination with the Abominable Snowman, first sparked by his father's bedtime stories, still smoldered. He decided to mount one more expedition to search for the "missing link", this time to the Pacific Northwest, where legends of Big Foot were common. He organized a trip that would be a family adventure, including sons Tom and Chuck, aged twelve and ten, and longtime partners in exploration, Peter Byrne and Travis Richardson.

"He said 'I know you are skeptical Travis,'" Richardson remembered, "and if I am having the wool pulled over my eyes, I want you with me."

Forty years later, the old rancher is not so sure what they saw. He closes his eyes and describes a one-armed man named Red, who owned a very special dog that had been trained to hunt bears. Red claimed that his dog was fearless and would run anything, but when they came to tracks on an old logging road, the dog's hackles bristled and it refused to move down the trail. Everyone froze as the dog howled in fear and ran back towards camp.

"Who knows?" Richardson asks today.

During the next few years, others took up the search, most notably John Green and Bob Titmus, whose Pacific Northwest Expedition in 1961 was well-documented. Cryptozoologist Dr. Richard Greenwell has statistically analyzed some of the data at the University of Arizona and remains convinced of the expedition's credibility.

According to Greenwell, Green reported capturing clear "Bigfoot tracks" on slide film. He gave the undeveloped rolls to Titmus, who sent them on to Slick in Texas. More than forty years later, they have never been seen; they remain, like the supposed yeti thumb, part of a lingering mystery. Author Loren Coleman explored that mystery in 1989, when he published *Tom Slick and the Search for the Yeti*; and the annual Bigfoot Conference (in different locations each year) remains a forum for the latest theories and expedition news about the elusive creature.

The entry to the Slick Residence, designed by architect O'Neil Ford in 1958. (*Photo by Larry Pearlstone, courtesy of Ford, Powell & Carson, Architects.*)

Slick's showcase home housed an art collection with works by Pablo Picasso, Georges Braque, Georgia O'Keefe, and sculptor Isamu Noguchi. (*Betty Slick Moorman Photo Collection.*)

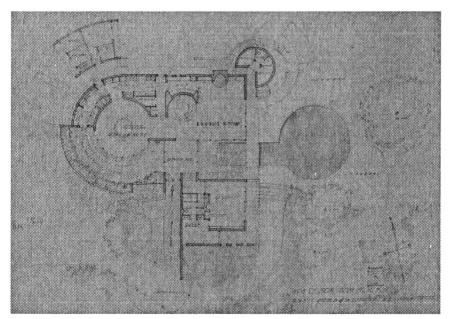

Architectural drawing of Slick Residence floorplan, by O'Neil Ford. (*Courtesy of Ford, Powell & Carson, Architects.*)

Slick loved the house's lush gardens and swimming pool; the large patio was perfect for entertaining his diverse friends who came from all over the world for his parties. (*Photo by Larry Pearlstone, courtesy of Ford, Powell & Carson, Architects.*)

Charles and Betty Urschel and "Curly" the boatman, in Port Aransas, Texas, where the Slick/Urschel families often gathered to fish and relax on the beach. (*Margaret Urschel Photo Collection.*)

The young Slicks and Urschels, first cousins and close friends, from left: Charles, Tom, and Patty Slick; Wendy and Margaret Urschel. (*Margaret Urschel Photo Collection.*)

Tom Slick with children Patty, Tom, and Chuck, 1959. (*Betty Slick Moorman Photo Collection.*)

The Slick Family on vacation in Sun Valley, Idaho, 1958. Left to right, Charles (Chuck), Tom, Patty, and father Tom. (*Photo courtesy of San Antonio Express News.*)

Tom Slick with oldest son, William Lewis Slick, and nephew, Jeff Moorman, 1959. (*Betty Slick Moorman Photo Collection.*)

C.V. Wood, Jr. (Woody) and his wife, actress Joanne Dru, shared Slick's love of mystery and imaginative ideas. Wood was an early partner in the development of Disneyland, helped Slick fund the Mind Science Foundation, started the famous Terlingua Chili Cook-Off in Texas and brokered a major merger for Warner Brothers. (*C.V. Wood Photo Collection, courtesy of the Mind Science Foundation.*)

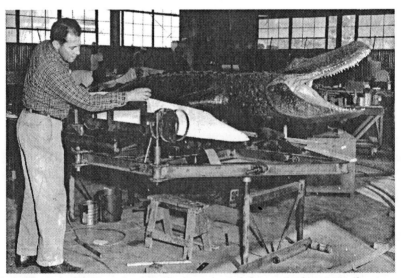

The early crocodiles at Disneyland were state-of-the art in the 1950s; forty years later Slick's Southwest Research Institute would be awarded the contract to make the new "skin" for the dinosaurs, crocodiles, and other creatures in the famous entertainment park. (*C.V. Wood Photo Collection.*)

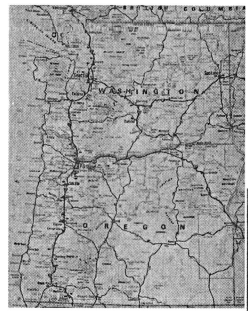

The Bigfoot expeditions of the late 1950s and early 1960s focused on the Cascade Mountain range in Oregon and Washington, in the Pacific Northwest. (*Peter Byrne Photo Collection.*)

Peter Byrne left the Himalayas in 1959 to organize Slick's Bigfoot expedition in the Pacific Northwest. His work continued there long after Slick's death; and his books, television appearances, and research remain a major source of information about the elusive creature. Here, Byrne examines the cast of a footprint at the Bigfoot Information Center, The Dalles, Oregon. (*Peter Byrne Photo Collection.*)

This controversial photograph was shot in 1960 in the woods of Northern California by an unknown photographer who left his film behind. Peter Byrne asked in his book, *The Search for Big Foot*, "was it a Bigfoot, or was it a hoax?" (*Peter Byrne Photo Collection.*)

157

Chapter Nine

Visions of the Future
(1955 – 1960)

W e prepare for war like precocious giants and for peace
like retarded pygmies," Eleanor Roosevelt wrote, quoting
her former associate in the United Nations, Canadian
Lester Pearson.

Tom Slick liked the quote and used it in his new book project,
and in the speech that he delivered at the World Peace Conference
in Paris in 1955. It produced a powerful visual image and he hoped
it would help drive the point, which was sometimes difficult when
discussing the somewhat esoteric concept of peace.

In 1951, Slick self-published his own blueprint for world peace,
calling it *The Last Great Hope*. For the next few years he tried to
influence his many friends in government and business to join the
effort; and he was thrilled to be invited to address the Paris conference
in 1955.

"This may well be the year for a dramatic – perhaps even a
decisive – advance in mankind's age-long quest for peace," Slick
said to the packed house in France, where the ravages of the war in
Europe just a decade before still were evident. An optimist in the
truest sense, he was certain that human beings really did want "lives
of order, unity and peace." And for the few who had not arrived at
this evolved state, he suggested that the horrors of modern war also
were powerful incentives to move forward in the peace process.

"The extreme horror of modern war, the blood-sucking drain of
the cost of armaments, and now the specter of atomic and hydrogen
destruction of whole populations, with other perhaps worse scientific terror weapons in the background, seem at last to have brought
a world-wide revulsion to these intolerable conditions which set the
stage, and condition the minds of men, everyplace, for some brave

new program to provide the machinery to prevent war," Slick wrote nearly fifty years ago.

He was premature. Military spending escalated; and nuclear weapons that were even more destructive were developed. The next decades would experience wars in Viet Nam, Central America, Sri Lanka, Kosovo and the Balkan States, the Middle East, several African nations, and Iraq.

Slick was not alone in his early peace efforts. He collaborated with Norman Cousins, the brilliant editor of *The Saturday Review*, on his research for *Permanent Peace*, the book published by Prentice Hall in 1958; and the two became personal friends. Slick respected Cousins's creative mind and ability to use his powerful networking and communication skills to really effect change. He also was openly admiring of the editor's home life, which appeared as full of projects and interesting people as Slick's, but also had a stability that Slick's did not.

"It was really a pleasure to visit you and Ellen at your home last weekend," he wrote, "and I think that you are to be envied your very fine way of life. You have a wonderful place, some wonderful children and I like the fine, interesting things that you do – such as your "Hiroshima maidens" deal."

Impressed by Cousins's concern for the victims of the Hiroshima bombing, in 1954 Slick adopted two Korean foster children through the Foster Parents Plan for War Children. Their names were Park Yong Kyu and Lee Yong Sook; and he regularly corresponded with them both until his death in 1962. Unlike many "foster parents" in the program who just sent their annual contributions, Slick established a real connection with the boys. He told them about his travels, his dreams, and the weather in Texas. He sent them magazines about science and his new peace book, as well as financial aid. His letters to them are an insight into the childlike sweetness that was such a part of the man.

Dear Park,

I was so happy to receive your very nice letter the other day. It certainly sounds like you had a wonderful time during your winter vacation. By your description I imagine Korea looks very pretty indeed with a blanket of snow covering it. You said you drew pictures of the snow scenery. Do you like to draw? I would like to see some of your drawings.

I have been traveling quite a bit lately. This summer my other Children and I are going to spend some time down at the coast swimming, fishing, and just relaxing in the sun.

My peace planning book is being printed right now, and I will send you a copy just as soon as it is finished. It is supposed to be completed in the fall.

How is your school work coming along? I know you are trying very hard to do your best and that pleases me very much. Write me again real soon and let me know how you are doing.

Affectionately, Your Foster Dad

As Slick traveled around the world during the first half of 1956, his mind was, as usual, whirling with new ideas and new tangents for his existing projects. He wrote again to Cousins, realizing that his friend was preparing to go to Africa to meet Dr. Albert Schweitzer.

"The greatest impression I've had on this round-the-world trip is that uncontrolled population increase is one of the world's URGENT problems … a good, cheap, practical technique to control reproduction, if available, would go a long way to solve the problem. Perhaps in Africa they might have a valuable lead.

"If you could find out more about on your trip, perhaps from Dr. Schweitzer, and obtain some material, I would arrange our foundation test it and do the chemical work necessary to turn it into a suitable product."

Just a few years later, the first oral contraceptives hit the market, developed and tested at Southwest Foundation in Texas. A decade later, the population explosion had gained the general public's attention, and the governments of China, India, Indonesia and others initiated new education programs, financial incentives, and contraceptive options to tackle this "urgent" problem.

161

Slick believed that "most of the world's urgent problems could be solved through Science and Peace"; and he understood that financial support for change was critical.

"Money is a useful tool," he told Cousins and others, urging them to join him in his unabashed solicitation of funds from anyone he could corner and convince to share his visions for the future.

As Cousins packed for Africa, Slick sent him still another suggestion. "…an interesting man to see down there would be the diamond king, Williamson, in Tanganyika. He reportedly is one of the wealthiest men in the world, and he apparently has no family nor plans for his great wealth. I am thinking that if you can meet with him, you might intrigue him with the idea of using some of his wealth for some important, worthwhile purposes…

"A bachelor geologist with a huge diamond mine in the middle of Africa might be the source of finances for Peace and Progress through Science!"

The son of the "king of the wildcatters" did not find anything intimidating about picking up the telephone or his pen to contact the "diamond king". Partly because he had enjoyed wealth, and the access that accompanies it, all of his life, Slick was never embarrassed about asking for what he wanted. Whether he was writing the Indian government about monsoor fish or David Rockefeller about joining his peace initiative, he was at ease, practicing the "nothing ventured, nothing gained" philosophy that he had learned from his father so many years ago.

This carried over to his personal life as well. Women who dated him during his bachelor days, and those who chose not to for one reason or another, remember that he never gave up. "Like clockwork, he would check in every few months," says a former girlfriend in New York. "I always was hoping that I'd be an 'exclusive' interest, but Tom was completely honest about his feelings and he was a fun, thoughtful friend. Of course, he had friends like me all over the world."

His letters prove it. They are extremely courteous, almost formal in their wording. They never allude to anything improper, and are not very personal, almost as if he thought the world might read them someday. They are most often responses to letters he had received, or notes of thanks for lovely weekends during his travels all over the world. A Christmas list went to Texas's most exclusive women's store, Neiman Marcus; sometimes Slick asked owner Stanley Marcus to select a gift for a special lady of the moment; and apparently Marcus was happy to do so.

Annette, Cathy, Cheryl, Cynthia, Irene, Jeanne, Jeri, Mary, Nancy, Nell, Sandra, Sylvia, Toni, Topsy, and three different women named Helen were on the 1958 holiday list; packages from Neiman Marcus were shipped to Australia, Beirut and Paris, across the United States to Arizona, California, New York, Oklahoma, and all over Texas.

"Every time he called for a date, and I refused because I was seeing someone else, he was never offended or angry," a San Antonio woman recalls forty-five years later. "But he never stopped calling. The word 'no' was just not in his vocabulary."

His former sister-in-law, Linda Nixon Seeligson agrees. "Success and failure never much concerned him," she says. "It was the quest that interested him. He was willing to back, with money and prestige, anyone who came to him with an idea, even when others found it 'bogus'.

"I remember a man who claimed he had found the essence of life. It was a clear liquid in a glass vial. Extensive time and research were expended on this; Tom never feared the perceptions of others; he was never afraid of seeming foolish."

This quality of deep self-confidence is rare in our achievement-oriented society, where tremendous value is placed on "fitting in" and social approval. Psychologists agree that a large number of their clients are drawn to therapy by fears of rejection, failure, and appearing foolish. And anyone who has raised a hand to answer a question in a schoolroom, invited someone to the prom, applied for a job, asked for raise, made a speech, or walked into an important event dressed "wrong" probably has felt that flutter of apprehension, pounding heart, and pure fear.

How did Slick escape it? Perhaps it started with his early lesson in the Clarion woods, when his father encouraged him to cross the river on a fallen log. Perhaps it was the early death of his father, forcing Slick to become "the man of the family" at just fourteen years old. Perhaps he innately understood what an important part of happiness this characteristic was. Liberated from the fear of failure and the limitations imposed by the perceptions of others, Slick never wallowed in past disappointments. Instead, he turned his attention to problems at hand, and always looked to the future.

Children were, of course, an important part of that future. His devotion to his daughter and three sons is highlighted in the hundreds of letters he wrote to them, about them, and to their mothers and teachers. Juggling his projects and exotic travels with his ex-wives' plans and antics in order to spend maximum time with Bill ("Wid"), Patty, Tom, and Charles (who later preferred "Chuck") was not easy. But, as in other endeavors, he was persistent. Whenever his two ex-wives, Betty Young and Polly Pater, weren't responsive to his plans, he simply called or wrote again and suggested an alternate plan.

A subscription to *Science Digest* and a set of golf clubs for Bill, an electric train (ordered from Macy's in New York for $5.95) for Tom, a Wonder Plane for Charles, a special manicure set and a cocker spaniel puppy for Patty – like most fathers, Slick was thoughtful in his gift selections for his children, checking with their mothers to see what they needed and wanted, asking friends for advice.

He wrote to Jim Searle, manager of the Lake Placid Club, where the family had spent their summer vacation in 1957, for advice, explaining:

> *"My little daughter is very anxious to have a cocker spaniel puppy but I have never cared for them because so many of them seem dumb. However, yours appeared bright and smart and most satisfactory. If this is true, I would appreciate your letting me know where I could obtain one like it. As this would be a Christmas present for her, I would appreciate hearing from you just as quickly as possible. Thanks very much and kindest regards."*
>
> Tom Slick

He harnessed his imagination to plan family trips to places that would appeal to children. The Slicks fished at the Texas Coast, spent time with their cousins in the mountains of Roaring Gap, North Carolina, shook hands with Mickey Mouse at Disneyland, watched surfing contests in Hawaii, went to the top of the Empire State Building in New York City, and later, went camping in the Pacific Northwest, where Slick was searching for "Bigfoot".

In addition to generous gifts and travel, and perhaps more important, he gave his children encouragement and advice despite long separations from them. His regular "love letters" to them told them how important they were; and they are the only letters in the collection that do not mention his diverse projects, theories, ideas for new ventures or world vision. Instead, Slick used the letters to focus his vision completely on the young children who missed him and the future adventures they would share.

Dear Bill,

I certainly enjoyed the visit with you in Dallas the other day. I am real proud of the way you are growing up and developing into a fine young man. Your mother wrote to me the other day that you are making fine progress in school and that she has received fine reports from your teachers.

I was very pleased to hear you say the other day that you think you would be interested in becoming a scientist. I believe that this would be a most interesting career and one in which you could accomplish a great deal of constructive work, which would give you a very interesting and gratifying life...

For this summer, your plans to work on your grandfather's ranch sound like they would be most interesting. I am sure you will enjoy it and get a lot out of the experience. However, it is easy to get hurt at that sort of work, and you are a little young for it, so I hope that you will be careful and cautious, particularly until you get used to it. I sent your saddle to you in care of your Uncle Bill.

We are looking forward to having you come down and visit us a little later in the summer so let me know as soon as you are ready to come down to San Antonio...we could all go down to the Coast for a while. Then, we have a camping and fishing

trip up in the mountains of Wyoming with your Uncle Lew and
Jeff...which will get you back in time to start school...
So have a wonderful summer and be careful not to get hurt. We
will be looking forward to seeing you a little later on.

Love, Dad

Other children in his extended family were important to Slick as well; he always approached them with total attention and a tenderness for the young that had been a part of his nature since childhood. His siblings and younger cousins remember him as a thoughtful, gentle hero.

Arthur Seeligson, his first cousin, was four years younger than Slick; his childhood memories of times spent together were precious more than seventy years later.

"Tom's father had just died; and my family moved into the Slicks' house in Oklahoma City," Seeligson explained shortly before his own death in 2001 at age eighty. "My mother was the youngest sister of Tom's mother; and my father was the attorney for the Estate. Back in the 1930s, it was very common for families to 'circle the wagons' in times like that."

The fourteen-year-old Slick took his younger cousin hunting and fishing, shared boyhood secrets, and treated him as an equal, earning his lifelong admiration and love. Eventually they would marry sisters; and while Slick's marriage did not last, everyone would remain "family" for the rest of their lives.

"It's hard to describe Tom's special charisma," eighty-year-old Seeligson said with a wistful smile. "When he was in a room, there was a sort of magical energy around him. He was very present in each moment; and all of us around him got the benefit of that."

Many others – children and adults – also felt that energy. Nieces and nephews, godchildren, and friends of all ages each have some story about the man who was a interesting combination of Santa Claus, the Pied Piper, and Mr. Wizard, weaving together an array of amazing toys, the elusive promise of adventure to exotic places, and of course, the excitement of science.

Slick was an early proponent of equal opportunity, and envisioned a future when all children would have the same chances in the world. In 1953, he wrote to Harold Vagtborg, the director of his scientific institutes, to share his views.

"Dr. S.D. Kane, Principal of Booker T. Washington Elementary School, is a fine Negro scholar and an able man. In my opinion, our institutions will be better off if we can add different races to our staff. With this in mind, several years ago I suggested to Dr. Kane that if he found any outstanding Negro scientists, we would like to consider them.

"He now has a young man, Charles W. Johnson, who will graduate from MIT in a couple of years with a degree in mathematics. He is interested in coming back to San Antonio and the possibility of a position at the Institute ... we could be a catalyst for his dream."

Today, the letter is not extraordinary, and even slightly "politically incorrect" with its use of the word "Negro" instead of "African American", which became preferred long after Slick's death. But in the context of the times, it is important.

Slick's own dream – rich, complex, and intertwined with perhaps thousands of related ideas – envisioned a future where science would make the world a better place. In an open letter addressed to "the Young People of Texas", which was circulated to various schools in the mid-1950s, he calls scientific research "the great open frontier of the future". He describes advances in agriculture (synthetic fertilizers, hybrid crops, and conservation were all brand new ideas), communications (television had just been invented), new materials (plastic had never been seen before), and space exploration (Russia had just put the first rocket in space) as examples of the results produced by science.

When the Russians unexpectedly launched "Sputnik" in 1957, the world's space program was born; and Slick was worried that the United States needed a drastic revitalization of its economy to compete, with more funds in the national budget allocated to basic research and development.

He wrote to friends in high political positions, including President Dwight Eisenhower, expressing his concerns that the Russians, British, and Germans were ahead in the international race for economic advancement, suggesting that America was dangerously complacent.

"Perhaps forthcoming developments will prove that our conviction that we lead the world technologically is not correct. If this is true, we should be the first to the know the facts; and if it takes a jolt to wake us up, the presence of the unwelcome terrestrial visitor with its living passenger circling unbidden in our skies, may serve the role of a most useful Paul Revere to warn us of danger in time to take counteracting measures."

Slick's correspondence was always answered; and Eisenhower considered the Slick/Urschel/Seeligson clan to be good friends. Once stationed at the U.S. Army's Fort Sam Houston in San Antonio, "Ike" and First Lady "Mamie" were frequent visitors to their beautiful mansions in Olmos Park; and while the possibility of visitors from another planet did not receive much public comment from the President, he amassed quite a collection of classified material on the subject in the 1950s.

Closer to home, however, was the knowledge that scientific advances would improve our world; and Slick was fervent and articulate on the subject.

"If we can continue to train young men and women who will advance the physical progress of our civilization through the powerful agency of scientific research, and at the same time add to our civilization the moral discipline necessary to properly utilize the advances, we could move our world forward, further in the next few years than in all of mankind's previous history.

"We have the instruments for progress in scientific research and, if we can solve our other problems such as justice, maintaining world peace, and other essential moral elements, we have before us a promising future indeed. The possibilities are definitely here – it is up to the men and women of the future to turn these potentialities into realities."

Prentice Hall published Tom Slick's *Permanent Peace* in 1958.

Tom Slick dreamed of creating a "Science City" at ESSAR Ranch, where his research institutes were attracting scientists and hosting conferences on world peace. He proposed partnering with developer Richard Gill to build a residential subdivision on 800 acres of the property to provide housing for the scientific communitiy. (*Photo courtesy of the Mind Science Foundation.*)

"It has always been my intention to work toward the building up of a greater center for human progress through scientific research." Tom Slick, 1960

When Southwest Research Institute celebrated its fiftieth anniversary in 1997, some of the scientists designed and built a prototype of "The Red Car" to symbolize a characteristic for which their institute's founder was famous. Slick developed what he called "the red car technique" in his earliest days of hiring outstanding people to join his various endeavors. First he got to know his chosen candidate, paying careful attention to any special desires that person expressed. He called those special hopes "the red car"; and they were usually far more appreciated by the new employee than a real red car. He almost always got a "yes" from the person he was pursuing when he used this technique. (*Photo by Bill Mallow, Southwest Research Institute.*)

Chapter Ten

The Unending Search
(1962 - ?)

It had been a wonderful week. Tom Slick had joined good friends and oil business colleagues in Calgary, Canada, for some excellent pheasant hunting. The camaraderie and interesting conversations had once again pushed his creative mind into uncharted places, and he was looking forward to pursuing some new projects as a result.

On October 6, 1962, he flew south from Canada, towards sunny Arizona, where he planned to have dinner with two of his children – Tom and Chuck – who now lived in Scottsdale with their mother. Then, the following week he would fly to the East Coast, to see the other two – Bill, who was attending Princeton University, and "little Patty", who was away at Miss Porter's, a boarding school in Connecticut. He had purchased tickets for the Yale/Princeton football game, wondering which team his daughter would cheer, with a "Yalic" for a father and her older brother at Princeton.

As Slick thought about upcoming plans, the weather worsened over Montana. He and the pilot discussed landing and waiting for the storms to end, but they seemed fairly scattered and fear was not a part of Slick's personality. As was his practice, he focused his mind on positive thoughts.

The next four months would be hectic. He planned to squeeze in a quick trip to India and the Himalayas in late October, returning to New York by November 7 to host a major peace conference. In the past week he had written to Professor K.T. Jahagirdar's colleague in Bombay, Nyaya Sharma, excited about the new psychic phenomena the man had reported witnessing firsthand. He was anxious to learn more; and meanwhile, he was practicing the meditation techniques that Sharma had taught him.

"My meditation is going considerably better," he wrote to the Indian, "although I must say that under conditions of my life here I am not carrying it out as regularly as I would like. One interesting thing that has happened is the regular occurrence to me in my mind of the route into your apartment. I absolutely picture the journey, with each turn, from the turn at the corner of the theatre, past the theatre into your street, into your building, into the elevator, out of the elevator on your floor, around to your door and into your apartment, and then into your private room to our sitting place with a clear picture of the group that met there."

Now Slick's mind followed the twists of his meditation as the plane lurched; and Shelly Sudderth, his pilot, followed the twists of the Beechcraft Bonanza 35 with increased concern. Sometime in the early evening of Saturday, October 6, the plane crashed over Montana's southwestern mountains, about forty miles south of Dillon.

Harold Briggs, search and rescue coordinator for the Montana Aeronautics Commission, said the plane appeared to have gone to pieces in flight, possibly as a result of an explosion or lightning. Wreckage was strewn of a three-quarter-mile area; and the bodies of Slick and Sudderth were found alongside a country road, nearly a mile from the center of the crash site.

By Monday morning, news of the accident appeared in the front page banner headline in his hometown newspaper, *The San Antonio News*, and other newspapers and magazines across the country also carried the story. The Slick children had lost a father; people from Texas to Tibet had lost a "best friend"; and the world had lost a true mystery hunter. Or had it?

"I plan to work just as hard on the other side," Slick told Jeri Walsh, his long time personal assistant and sometimes girlfriend, and Bill Rhame, his confidante and CEO of Texstar Corporation, both of whom had become ardent supporters of Slick's newest research institute, the Mind Science Foundation. Both Walsh and Rhame were convinced, until their own deaths several decades later, that Tom Slick's quest continued, in another dimension. It definitely continued in this world.

With the start of the twenty-first century and the new millennium, there is tremendous interest in the possibility of other dimensions, life beyond our planet, the vast undiscovered potential of the human mind, and other mysteries that Tom Slick investigated. The search certainly has not ended.

On December 29, 1999, *The Washington Post* announced, "What the millennium holds may be in one's mind," as part of its series *The Next 1000 Years*. According to the cover story, some of the brightest scientists and philosophers in the world today think that the human mind and brain are the final frontier. Slick certainly would agree.

Joseph Dial, Executive Director of Slick's youngest organization, the Mind Science Foundation, is convinced that empirical research is at last "catching up" with Slick's 1958 mission to understand the way the brain and mind work. In 2004, the Foundation established the Tom Slick Research Awards for Consciousness, to recognize and support some of those nascent discoveries.

The first award winners include Baroness Susan Greenfield, Ph.D., an Oxford University professor of Neuropharmacology, and Director of the Royal Institution of Great Britain; Christopher Koch, Ph.D., a neuro-physicist at California Technical Institute,, in charge of the Neural Computation Laboratory, collaborating with Nobel Laureate Sir Francis Crick on the links between visual perception and imagination; J. Allan Hobson, M.D., from Harvard Medical School, specializing in dreams as a window to consciousness; Elizabeth Lloyd Mayer, Ph.D., at the University of California-Berkeley, working to develop aspects of "Coincidence Theory," which was named by the *New York Times* as one of the "67 most exciting ideas for 2003"; Steven Laureys, M.D., Ph.D., working at the Cyclotron Research Center in Belgium; and Abraham Verghese, M.D., MFA, who has recently added a center for medical humanities and ethics to the study of medicine at the University of Texas Health Science Center in San Antonio, Texas. Already identified for the next awards are Jeffrey Schwartz, M.D., a neuro-psychiatrist at the University of California Los Angeles, who is studying self-directed neuroplasticity (or, in plain English, the ability to change the brain through things like meditation); and V. Ramashandran,

M.D., Ph.D., author of *The Artful Brain*, specializing in the neuro-humanities at the University of California San Diego.

Dial believes that "brain science will be the next genetics, revealing the very essence of ourselves", and like Slick, likes pushing the boundaries. One of the Foundation's newest projects, planned for 2005, is a CD on consciousness, being produced by Dr. Bernard Barrs, a cognitive psychologist at the Neurosciences Institute in La Jolla, California. The fact that it will be included as a part of college level introductory Psychology textbooks is remarkable evidence that the scientific community is at last paying attention to some of the fundamental questions about the human mind and its potential.

Visionary author and futurist Arthur Clarke (*2001: A Space Odyssey*) has suggested that the next decades will include a human landing on Mars, and that "infra-red signals will be detected coming from the center of the Galaxy, the product of a technologically advanced civilization." Slick suggested the same thing in his 1953 letter to President Eisenhower, noting the importance of our nation's new space program.

Explorers like marine biologist Sylvia Earle are using deep submersibles to plumb the ocean depths for new discoveries; and evidence of a Giant Squid in the deep Mariana Trench off New Zealand provides an adventure every bit as exciting as Slick's search for the yeti in the Himalayas. There is a certain degree of serendipity in the fact that Southwest Research Institute is developing and testing the deep rovers that will make these new journeys to the bottom of the sea possible.

Clarke has predicted that nano-technology will eventually produce a "universal replicator," allowing us to create any object, however complex, if scientists are given the necessary raw material and information matrix. "Diamonds or gourmet meals can literally be made from dirt," he explained as the new millennium dawned.

Slick liked both diamonds and good food; and his Southwest Research Institute already is creating some amazing products from dirt and even waste, including a new building material called Xorax.

As futurists imagine what is ahead, the institutions established in the 1940s and 1950s by Tom Slick already have provided many of the breakthroughs and tools that will take us there.

The Southwest Foundation for Biomedical Research (SFBM), established in 1941, has pursued basic scientific and medical research for more than sixty years, expanding from its original core group of six scientists working in an un-airconditioned ranch house to a staff of two hundred on a twelve-hundred-acre campus that houses a state-of-the-art Level Four bio-containment laboratory and the new Southwest Regional Primate Center, home to the largest baboon colony in the world.

Tom Slick first became interested in "apes," a group of primates in which he included chimpanzees, baboons, and orangutans, during a 1952 safari in Kenya with famous white hunter Bunny Allen. He was charmed by the mischievous antics and human-like expressions of the chimps; and at night, several pet monkeys always joined the hunters around the campfire.

As dinner and drinks were served, conversation drifted to the historic lore of ancient Africa; and Allen told Slick that in 1630 a live chimpanzee was supposedly sent by an African chief to the Prince of Orange in the Netherlands. Europe was "horrified and enthralled by the creature," according to reports; and by the end of the seventeenth century, Edward Tyson, one of England's best known anatomists wrote that "a chimpanzee resembles Man in many of its Parts, more than any of the Ape-kind, or any other Animal in the world."

Returning from his adventures in Africa, Slick suggested to the scientists at Southwest Foundation that non-human primates might provide a valuable research model for their investigations of heart disease. And few years later, the emerging U.S. space program used a chimpanzee as the first passenger in the Mercury capsule because it was the animal most like humans biologically.

Thirty years after Slick's death, DNA studies established the genetic similarity between humans and primates at 96.4 percent or higher, and by the end of the twentieth century, Southwest Foundation's primate research had become a vital scientific resource, producing breakthroughs in heart disease, neonatal complications, infectious diseases, osteoporosis, cancer, and a wide variety of other human conditions.

In the 1950s and 1960s, steroid research and hormone metabolism led to new treatments for hypertension, atheriosclerosis, and cardiopulmonary disease. Research by Goldzieher and Alexrod resulted in the first drugs for contraception, fulfilling Slick's earlier hopes for new interventions that could be used for population planning; and Rao's development of various anti-hormones as tumor inhibitors further established the Foundation's scientific standing, both nationally and internationally .

Testing of new vaccines began in the 1960s, and the first successful vaccines for hepatitis B, and later hepatitis A, were developed at the Foundation. More than thirty vaccines for HIV have been tested in chimpanzees; at least two are currently in large scale clinical trials.

In 1976, Duncan Wimpress, Ph.D., former president of Trinity University, was selected to lead the Foundation. His fundraising skills had catapulted Trinity to new national levels; and the Board was confident he would help the Foundation in the same way. In 1979, under Wimpress's leadership, a new department of Genetics was established to focus on this burgeoning new field of research. Soon, it proved the important role of genetics in arterial lesions and hypercholesterolemia. It developed research models for studying chronic lung disease in infants, and produced the first-generation high frequency ventilator for its treatment.

By the 1980s, investigations of spinal cord injuries and repair techniques were underway; and a unique model of melanoma was yielding new treatment options for this deadly form of cancer.

The 1990s brought the development of the first non-human primate gene map, parallel to the human genome project, which led to even better identification of the genes that influence susceptibility to diseases, and new strategies for preventing and treating them. When Wimpress retired in 1992, Frank Ledford M.D., who served as Surgeon General for the U.S. Army from 1988 until 1992, assumed the presidency of the Foundation. His national prominence in medical, scientific, and military circles added still more stature to the Foundation's growing international reputation.

In 2001, construction of a Level Four bio-containment laboratory gave the Foundation the super-technology it needed to study some of the deadliest infectious diseases on the planet, including *Ebola, Dengue,* and *Hantas* virus; and the Southwest Regional Primate Research Center was established in 2002, building on the Foundation's many years of primate research to provide infrastructure and resources for new national collaborations and much greater impact on national progress in biomedical research. In 2005, Ledford retired; and Dr. Anthony Infante was appointed to the Foundation's presidency in June. Leadership positions at the University of Texas Health Science Center at San Antonio, the Children's Immunology Clinic at Santa Rosa Children's Hospital, and the Children's Cancer Research Center position Infante for a smooth transition and continuation of the growth that the Foundation enjoyed during Ledford's tenure. Chair of Board, John Kerr, describes Infante as "a world-class scientist with a body of research spanning thirty years and a long track record of successful organizational leadership."

The Southwest Research Institute (SwRI), established by Slick in 1947, now employs more than twenty-five hundred people, including one thousand scientists, and is the third largest applied research facility in the world. Working for clients that range from the United States government and American corporations to individual inventors and international companies, SwRI has developed products that have improved our world, just as Slick hoped it would.

Automobile airbags, time-released medicine, polymers for dental appliances, germ-killing paint, Liquid Paper, bar-code readers, and rocket engines are just a few of the diverse inventions that have changed our lives in the last fifty years, fulfilling Slick's early published claim that "no problem or plan is too small or too large for consideration by the Institute."

From its modest beginnings at Essar Ranch, in the eighteen-room house that Slick had called home before moving to nearby San Antonio, hoping that his young wife would be less lonely there, Southwest Research Institute grew to encompass more than two million square feet of building space, with annual revenues that exceed three hundred million dollars.

Each year, *R&D Magazine* presents special awards to the hundred most technologically significant new products. The *Chicago Tribune* calls the awards "the Oscars of invention"; and Southwest Research Institute has received more than twenty-five in the last twenty years. A few of the advances selected for recognition include the PSI Meritor tire inflation system, weather environment simulation technology (WEST), self-restoring traffic barriers, fire resistant diesel fuel, a seismic velocity logging probe, the SUB-ICE icebreaking engine, and a new Sulphlex paving material that prevents the formation of potholes in roadways.

Since the initiation of the Clean Air Act of 1963, SwRI has helped set automotive emission standards by developing tests that measure fuel and emission characteristics, and by building new engines and exhaust after-treatment methods that reduce emissions. Development of underwater research submersibles during the same timeframe provided research pioneers of the deep waters to explore new worlds; and new space flight instruments have taken astronauts to new frontiers on the moon and beyond. The Cassini spacecraft, launched in 1997 for an eleven-year mission to the Saturn system, carries two instruments developed at SwRI to study the chemical makeup of that far off galaxy.

New techniques of microencapsulation, invented at SwRI, have been critical for more effective drug delivery; and the food industry is currently using this technology to add "nutraceuticals" to consumer products, and to add shelf-life to certain foods.

Southwest Research Institute's first sizable contract, in 1948, was to help a chemical company on the Gulf Coast of Texas treat its factory waste. And fifty years later, materials scientist Bill Mallow still was experimenting with waste, and ways to use it in productive ways around the world, eventually producing Xorax, a lightweight building material made from treated waste.

From the outset, leaders linked the Institute's work to the growing petroleum and agriculture industries in Texas. Evaluating and testing lubricants, computer simulation of pipeline-pumping systems, and other energy-related projects provided a steady source of income that continues today.

SwRI quickly outgrew its laboratories in the old Cable House, and by its tenth anniversary it employed 450 people, and reported rcvcnucs of $4.5 million. In 1955, Slick hired Martin Goland, an aerospace engineer who had been Director of Engineering Sciences at Midwest Research Institute, in Kansas City, Missouri, to head the Institute's technical program; his vision eventually would help shape the future and expand the scope of the Institute.

During the mid-1950s, Slick's early vision of a Science City was becoming a reality; and ESSAR Ranch was living up to its name as a place where science and research ("SR") lived in productive co-existence.

But the Institute of Inventive Research (IIR) was proving difficult to manage, largely due to the challenges involved with verifying the origin of hundreds of inventions and ideas for inventions that poured in, and the growing demands and impacts produced at the other two institutions. While it had produced some remarkable new products, including the "Thirsty Kerchief", a hooded hair-dryer that women could use at home, and the Lift Slab method of construction, which offered building contractors a new efficiency in building, Vagtborg convinced Slick that IIR's functions could be absorbed by the faster-growing SwRI; and in 1957, it was closed.

By 1959, Slick realized that the Foundation and SwRI had grown too big for just one president. Vagtborg remained at the helm of the Foundation; and Goland was promoted to president of SwRI, move that has been called a turning point for the Institute.

"Goland raised the sights of people working here so they thought more broadly," General Austin Betts, former Senior Vice President for Operations, explained. Scientists were urged to integrate their disciplines; and the Institute began to break away from its early regional focus.

Goland remained president until his death in 1997, when he was succeeded by J. Dan Bates, formerly the Executive Vice President for Finance. While SwRI's first leadership came from fields of science, Bates brought a new fiscal focus to the organization. In the past, success at SwRI was measured by how much good science and engineering was developed there; today, financial growth is an important factor as well. Bates is pursuing new opportunities with Asian clients, recognizing the growth in those economies; and SwRI recently completed the design for a huge, six-thousand-horsepower diesel locomotive engine for Chinese government as part of a new multi-million dollar contract.

Even more recently, scientists developed three-dimensional cellular imaging techniques to assess the pharmacological value of new cancer drugs competing for federal approval. With more than fifteen thousand new compounds being created annually, there is a growing bottleneck at the evaluation level, with only one compound every two to four years being deemed effective enough to promote to clinical trials. This new screening method uses a light-scattering technique to analyze the structure and composition of matter, enabling scientists to define the efficacy or potency of a new drug, and to determine whether animal testing is warranted.

Before the Iraq war began in 2003, the U.S. Army awarded SwRI a six million dollar contract to upgrade the CH-47 "Chinook" helicopter fleet. A medium-lift helicopter, used to haul ammunition and artillery, petroleum, troops and other cargo for the Army. Since its fielding in 1962, increasing problems developed in the craft, threatening to ground the fleet. Scientists analyzed prior failures and improved the helicopter's reliability in time for use in Iraq in 2003. The helicopter project would undoubtedly have appealed to Slick's interest in aviation and his patriotism; but he would have been disappointed to learn that his dreams of worldwide peace were still not coming true.

His research on the subject occupied much of his time from the middle 1950s until his death. In addition to publishing two books on the economic and social advantages of world peace, he created a means to lend his support in the future, by creating the Tom Slick Chair for World Peace at the University of Texas, in Austin, to be funded after his death.

Now a part of the Lyndon B. Johnson School at UT, the funding has underwritten symposia on the implications of sustainable development on world peace, and think tanks to disseminate the latest information on dollars being spent on fighting around the world. In 2003, Montgomery C. Meigs, a retired U.S. Army General, was selected by the University to occupy the Chair's professorship.

Meigs left active duty on January 1, 2003, after a six year command of all Army forces in the ninety-one-country area of responsibility of the U.S. European Command. Experiences during the Vietnam War, Operation Desert Storm, and two tours of peace-keeping duty in Bosnia made Meigs a powerful voice for articulating the complexities of both war and peace. Like Slick, he saw the truth in Eleanor Roosevelt's quote about preparing for war like giants, and for peace like pygmies; and in 2004, with the Iraq war raging, the world seemed to recognize that sustainable peace efforts must become global and top priority.

World peace, like every mystery that Tom Slick pursued, proved elusive. But that never stopped Slick; in fact he increased his efforts when others said things could not be done. His legacy of inventions, discoveries, and unanswered questions still continues at the institutions he established, and resonates with new mystery hunters of the twenty-first century.

On October 6, 1962, Tom Slick was killed in an airplane crash over Montana. Wire services carried the story across the United States and beyond. (*Newspaper cover courtesy of* San Antonio Express *Collection.*)

In addition to numerous stories about Tom Slick's accomplishments in the worlds of business and science, hundreds of letters were received by his sister and other family members citing diverse acts of kindness and friendship. An anonymous friend sent this to the San Antonio paper for publication. (*Betty Slick Moorman Photo Collection, courtesy of the* San Antonio Express.)

Tribute to Tom Slick

Dear Sir:

Much space and time and many beautiful and sincere tributes will be accorded Tom Slick during the days ahead. All will be richly deserved. There is still one more facet in Tom's full though tragically brief life which has not been touched on, and that is the love that Tom had for children and the love that they had for him.

Tom and I took our children on many outings during the years, and they learned from him many wonderful and important things about nature and hunting and fishing and good sportsmanship. For my part, each of these happy occasions inspired me to be a better and a more understanding father, because Tom was the best father I have ever known.

Always a loving disciplinarian, he never pampered his children, but he enriched their lives and those of my own children with memories that they will cherish forever.

My children were riding just before the sad news was flashed, one of them on a beautiful palomino that was a gift from Tom. When they returned home and saw the grief written on our faces an amazing thing happened. Our eldest daughter broke into tears and cried "What has happened? Is it Uncle Tom?" How could she have known? I am very close to my daughter and my own guess is that she didn't know at all; she was simply expressing a grief-inspired fear. Clearly we had just lost somebody very dear to us; the last person in the world she wanted it to be was naturally the name that came to her lips first.

Of all the tributes to Tom, the most touching of all could be made by the children in Tom's life—his own children and the friends of his children, and the children of his friends. And I think that is the way Tom would want it to be.

Name Withheld

184

Slick's mother and stepfather, Berenice and Charles Urschel, Sr., c. 1962.
(*Margaret Urschel Photo Collection.*)

Aerial Photo of Southwest Foundation, April 2005. The first scientific research institute created by Tom Slick in 1941 was Southwest Foundation for Biomedical Research. It has grown from six scientists working in a few un-airconditioned buildings to a campus that now houses the largest research primate colony in the world. (*Photo courtesy of Southwest Foundation for Biomedical Research.*)

Dr. Pemmaraju N. Rao was one of the early scientists at Southwest Foundation. Now Chair of the Department of Organic Chemistry, and a Trustee of the Mind Science Foundation, Dr. Rao remembers his first un-airconditioned lab in the old Cable House facility. (*Photo by Clem Spalding, courtesy of Southwest Foundation for Biomedical Research.*)

186

In 1999, the National Institutes of Health designated SFBR as the country's eighth National Primate Research Center. The Foundation is home to approximately 6,000 nonhuman primates, including the largest research colony of baboons in the world. Just as Slick hypothesized in the 1950s, primates have been proven to have a close similarity to humans in both genetics and physiology, filling a critical role in efforts to understand human health and disease. (*Photo by Clem Spalding, courtesy of Southwest Foundation for Biomedical Research.*)

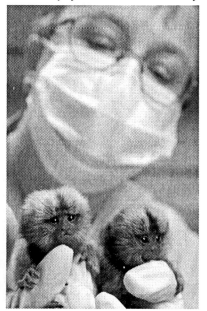

Maternal and child health, infectious diseases, cardiovascular health and natural processes of aging are just a few of the areas of research underway at SFBR; and primate models have enabled scientists to develop vaccines for Hepatitis A and B, experiment with treatments for Hepatitis C and HIV, to perfect fetal cardiac surgery, and to collaborate both nationally and internationally on a wide variety of health concerns. (*Photo by Clem Spalding, courtesy of Southwest Foundation for Biomedical Research.*)

187

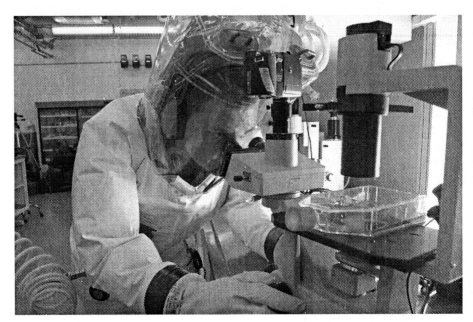

Scientists in the Department of Virology and Immunology are researching HIV and AIDS, Hepatitis C, emerging and exotic viruses including Dengue and Ebola, and new studies related to biodefense. Even before the anthrax attacks of 2001, SFBR was working with the University of Texas Austin to develop an antibody to treat the deadly toxins that are released by antrax bacteria during infection. (*Photo by Geno Loro, courtesy of Southwest Foundation for Biomedical Research.*)

SFBR virologists have some of the best-equipped facilities in the world, including the nation's only privately owned biosafety level four (BSL-4) laboratory, named the Betty Slick and Lewis J. Moorman, Jr. Laboratory, dedicated in 1999. This space-suit lab is designed for maximum containment so that scientists can safely study deadly pathogens for which there are no treatments or vaccines. (*Photo by Clem Spalding, courtesy of Southwest Foundation for Biomedical Research.*)

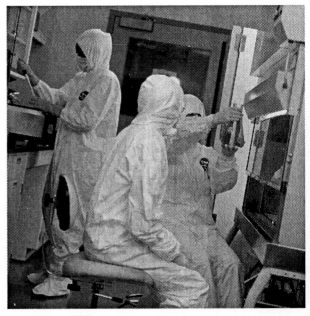

1953 aerial view of Southwest Research Insitute. (*Photo courtesy of Southwest Research Institute.*)

Southwest Research Institute® is an independent, nonprofit, applied engineering and physical sciences research and development organization using multidisciplinary approaches to problem solving. The Institute occupies 1,200 acres and provides nearly two million square feet of laboratories, test facilities, workshops, and offices for more than 3,000 employees who perform contract work for industry and government clients. (*Photo courtesy of Southwest Research Institute.*)

For the space shuttle Columbia accident investigation, SwRI recreated the impact scenario that occurred when a piece of insulating foam broke off the external fuel tank during launch. These tests indicated that a piece of foam punched a hole in the shuttle wing as shown in this photo. (*Photo courtesy of Southwest Research Institute.*)

SwRI developed this Microelectrome-chanical (MEMS) system to peer deep into the human body for information used to diagnose and treat a myriad of problems. Seen in a probe station used for testing, the one-centimeter-square chip contains more than 60 mechanical devices. (*Photo courtesy of Southwest Research Institute.*)

SwRI's 16,000-square-foot automotive fleet laboratory houses a four-wheel-drive chassis dynamometer that expands our fleet testing capabilities and accommodates the new generation of all-wheel-drive vehicles. It offers bumper-to-bumper fleet evaluations that provide vehicle manufacturers with proof of performance and comparative data. (*Photo courtesy of Southwest Research Institute.*)

Fleet testing in the early 1950s at Southwest Research Institute was on a much smaller scale, but no less important. (*Photo courtesy of Southwest Research Institute.*)

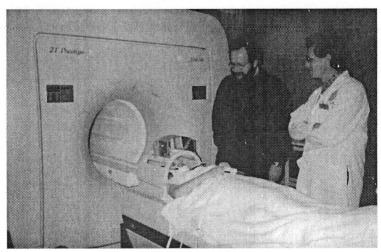

The Mind Science Foundation was the last scientific institute established by Tom Slick. Inspired by "unexplained phenomena" he encountered on his adventures in South America and the Himalayas, he wanted the scientific method applied to the mysteries of the mind. New technology like Positron Emission Tomography (PET) enables scientists to gather new information about how the brain works. Dr. John Murray directed MSF's Television Violence Project, using PET to study the brain's reaction to TV violence. (*Photo courtesy of the Mind Science Foundation.*)

The Tom Slick Research Awards in Consciousness were established by the Mind Science Foundation to recognize outstanding scientists and physicians who are advancing mind/brain consciousness work. Nationally renowned physician and author Dr. Abraham Verghese receives the 2004 award from executive director Joseph Dial, and is congratulated by Board members Paul Ingmundson, Ph.D. (left), Chairman Sandy McNab (second from right) and Emilio Romero, M.D. (far right). (*Photo by Ansen Seale, courtesy of the Mind Science Foundation.*)

Painted after Tom Slick's death in 1962, this portrait is displayed at the Mind Science Foundation. It depicts the diverse interests of a complex, mulit-faceted man. (*Courtesy of the Mind Science Foundation.*)

Epilogue
The Legacy

In April 1999, applause erupted as a figure in a bright blue space-suit lumbered over to the thick titanium door of the new Level Four bio-containment laboratory and slowly opened it. Inside, other similarly clad scientists would soon study the most terrible infectious diseases of the twenty-first century, hunting down mysterious microbes and pathogens that threaten our lives.

"If Tom Slick were alive, he'd be wearing one of those suits and a grin as big as Texas," a voice in the crowd whispered.

As the microbe hunters modeled their research battle gear, a cool April breeze softened the warmth of the Texas sun. World-famous scientists, board members, journalists, community leaders, and the family of Tom Slick gathered to cut a bright red ribbon, opening the newest laboratory at the Southwest Foundation for Biomedical Research.

The lab would begin its work the following month, in May, and family and old friends of Tom Slick remembered his May birthday and liked this celebration of sorts for a remarkable man who did not live to see his dream reach twenty-first century proportions.

Betty Slick Moorman walked slowly around the makeshift stage to the waiting ribbon. Still delicately beautiful at eighty-one years old, her eyes glistened slightly as she thought about her older brother, dead for nearly thirty-seven years, whose sometimes far-fetched dreams became realities like today's laboratory. She thought about her own husband, Lewis Moorman, Jr., dead only one year, a partner in all of her family's endeavors, the steady hand that raised Southwest Foundation to its position as a leading research center in the world. She smiled gently at her younger brother, Earl, seventy-seven years old, from Winston Salem, North Carolina, oilman and entrepreneurial founder of Slick Airways, confidante of his brother through every adventure, in Texas today for the dedication. With a special nod to her son-in-law, John Kerr, now Chairman of the Board of Southwest Foundation, she reached the ribbon. Sunlight illuminated the oversized scissors; and as the blades gleamed, she cut the scarlet banner and welcomed the crowd into the future.

"I would like to tell you how important the machinery of science is towards the future advancement of our civilization," Tom Slick wrote in 1952. *"Science gives us a tool of unparalleled effectiveness by which we can improve the physical side of our lives, and since science recognizes no boundaries, the lives of people all over the world."*

Certainly some of the deadliest threats the new lab would study are known worldwide, most notably in West Africa, South America, Mexico and Asia. Relative "newcomers" to Western researchers, emerging pathogens like *Dengue, Sabia, Ebola, Guanarito* and *Hantavirus* soon would be captured behind the heavy titanium doors; along with more familiar killers like the HIV virus which causes AIDS, and Hepatitis C, the terrible enemy of the liver that usually leads to fatal hepatocellular carcinoma. The space-suited team of microbe hunters was ready for them.

Demonstrating their specialized ventilation and waste management systems, full body suits with respiratory support, emergency backup breathing air tanks connected by spiraling yellow coils, and special showers of powerful disinfectants, they showed off their new protective tools with the rapture of small children on Christmas morning, waking to discover beneath the tree a shiny red miniature fireman's suit, the long-dreamed of chemistry set, or the newest robotic toy that Santa Claus could find. They smiled at the audience, and looked at the lab's shining door with anticipation, energized by the prospect of battling adversaries that would soon be inside.

The Tom Slick "formula" would soon be at work there, using the same ingredients that launched his Abominable Snowman/Yeti expeditions to investigate reports of evolution's "missing link" in the Himalayas, the Brangus project in 1948 to produce a heartier breed of cattle, the Liftslab construction program in 1954 to test a new engineering innovation that literally raised the roof on the building industry, and the "Special Mice" project in the mid-1950s to research early chemotherapies for cancer treatment. Tom Slick's formula always started with an unsolved mystery, a team of experts, a "capture" of sorts, a thorough investigation held to rigorous scientific standards, and finally, a sharing of the results whatever the outcome.

In a 1952 letter "to the Boys and Girls of Texas", Slick described the tremendous advances of science during the first fifty years of the twentieth century, noting that "probably greater advances have been made than the progress previously attained in the whole past ages of history." He predicted still more impressive breakthroughs by the year 2000.

Dr. Frank Ledford, former Surgeon General of the U.S. Army, and president of Southwest Foundation for Biomedical Research since 1985, squinted in the Texas sun, thinking about the remarkable discoveries he had witnessed in the last few decades in medicine, confirmation of Slick's prediction nearly fifty years ago. Many more would occur just inside the doors of this new thirty-four thousand square foot research building, named *the Betty Slick and Lewis J. Moorman, Jr., Laboratory* in honor of the sister and brother-in-law who had pursued Tom Slick's vision into the new millennium.

Tim Hixon, former Chairman of the Board, whose uncle had hunted big game with Slick in the 1940s, donated a wing, as did Dr. Burton Grossman, SBC Communications, and United Services Automobile Association (USAA), all generous corporate citizens with a history of supporting scientific research in Texas. Earl Slick made one of the largest gifts to the capital campaign, in honor of his brother, sister, and brother-in-law. A major grant from the National Institutes of Health (NIH), and funding from private donors from San Antonio and beyond – many with personal connections to Tom Slick, and Betty and Lew Moorman – started the Foundation's march into the future.

Dr. John VandeBerg, scientific director in 1999, led the new research flank of the march, recognizing that the beginning of a new millennium was a powerful catalyst, a time to bridge the old and the new.

"Who in the early twentieth century could have imagined the vaccine revolution that would enable us to prevent polio, typhoid, diphtheria, yellow fever, and so many other deadly diseases? Who, even as recently as 1950, could have imagined the genetics revolution and the technologies arising from it, that hold so much promise for our abilities to diagnose, treat, and prevent disease?" VandeBerg asked during the ceremony.

Who indeed? Probably Tom Slick.

As the crowd applauded on that lovely spring day in Texas, anticipating the discoveries that would emerge as the space-suited scientists explored their new mysteries, it glimpsed the dawn of the twenty-first century. From the adjoining primate center, baboons and chimpanzees joined the noisy salute with their own primal shouts; and more universal questions suddenly permeated the day, along with memories of a man who loved mystery and pursued those questions, always daring to journey into the wilderness of his intuition, to that creative place where no one else had ever been. A few in the audience heard the slow hum of a single-engine airplane; and glancing skyward, wondered if Tom Slick might be just beyond the horizon.

Acknowledgements

This five-year research and writing project has taken me on an incredible journey, allowing me to spend time with some remarkable people, and to take those roads less traveled, to some of the world's most remote places. I am deeply mindful that this book project has been a privilege and a joy in my life.

Tom Slick's family shared firsthand stories that were essential to the book; and I am especially grateful to Betty Slick Moorman for many extraordinary hours of interviews and reminiscing, as well as for access to her treasured collection of family photographs, many of which appear in this book. Thanks also to Earl Slick, Ramona Frates Seeligson, Arthur Seeligson, Jr., Linda Nixon Seeligson, Frates Seeligson, and Kent Frates for their wonderful insights about a remarkable man, to Margaret Urschel for photos from the Urschel Family collection, and to U.S. Congressman Lamar Seeligson Smith for loaning me his grandfather's copy of the 1934 book written by Joseph Frates (Tom Slick's grandfather) describing Slick's very first international adventure at the age of eighteen. Slick's children – Wid Slick, Patty Slick Beem, Tom Slick, and Chuck Slick – also were generous in their support of my efforts; and their childhood memories gave me important glimpses of their father through a different lens.

Tom Slick had friends all over the world, and many contributed interesting and exciting accounts of times they spent with a complex man they admired. Alphabetically, thanks to General Austin Betts, Peter Byrne, Nancy Cooke de Herrera, Josephine Gill, Joseph Goldzieher, M.D., Steven Juhasz, Ph.D., Bill Mallow, Ph.D., James W. Nixon, Jr., M.D., Jesse Oppenheimer, Esq., Pushkar Shumsher Jung Bahadu Rana, Pemmaraju Rao, M.D., Ph.D., William T. Rhame, Ph.D., Travis and Dorothy Richardson, Burleson Smith, Esq., Patsy Steves, Jeri Walsh, Robert V. West, Jr., Ph.D., and Duncan Wimpress,

Ph.D., for their stories, and in some cases, for some of the book's historic photographs.

I am grateful to several outstanding publishing professionals – Sandra Martin, my literary agent, who has been by my side from the project's start; Lisa Hagan, president of Paraview Press, who published the book; Morten Nilsen, the extraordinary designer who brought these pages to life with beautiful typeface and a graceful willingness to work with challenging old photos; Stephen Topping, a thoughtful editor who always respected the book's focus on mystery; and Larry Walker, publisher of the *San Antonio Express News* and Mira Pirezzo, president of Johnson Books, who both helped me navigate the perils of publishing. Nell Seeligson Smith conducted important background research for the project; Anson Seale transferred precious photos, some almost one hundred years old, to digital format; and Tom Parrish at Alamo Photo Labs produced the final print quality disk. Authors (and dear friends) Whitley Strieber, Anne Strieber, Johan Reinhard, and Jan Jarboe Russell shared their valuable publishing advice and counsel with me.

Institutions founded by Tom Slick added a critical dimension to my research; and the discovery of Slick's letters in a shed at Southwest Foundation for Biomedical Research enabled me to really probe the mind of a remarkable thinker. Special thanks to General Frank Ledford, M.D., president of SWFMR until 2005, and to John VandeBerg, Ph.D., first the foundation's scientific director and currently the director of its new primate facility, for opening the doors of their offices, laboratories, and storage shed. Scientists at Southwest Research Institute, some in their eighties and one over ninety years old, supplied firsthand accounts of early discoveries; and Joseph Dial, executive director of The Mind Science Foundation provided some glimpses of current and future research that Slick would love. Prior to Dial's leadership at MSF, I had the privilege to serve as that Foundation's executive director; and I am deeply grateful to the organization's Board of Directors for its strong support of the Tom Slick book project, both during my tenure at MSF and afterwards.

Thanks to the Explorers Club, The Mountain Institute, and Himalayan Holidays for nurturing my love of the Himalayas, and to the small team of good friends who accompanied me to Nepal in 2001 to search for the yeti (and the ghost of Tom Slick): Dan Bennett, Brian Hanson, Rima Lewis, Susan Taylor Rosepink, and Brad Towne, Ph.D.

Finally, there are always those very special people, who seem to miraculously intuit the perfect moment for an action that makes all things possible. Betty and Bob Kelso established the Catherine Nixon Cooke Chair for Exploration at The Mind Science Foundation in 1999; and that generous contribution allowed me to lead the yeti expedition to the Himalayas in 2001, interviewing the elderly porters who had traveled with Slick nearly fifty years before and certainly provided a unique perspective to the book. Close friends Kit and Angie Goldsbury also took me to the mountains, to their beautiful home in Aspen, Colorado, when I just couldn't seem to finish the last chapters of the book. Nestled in my fleece in the crisp air, watching bears come up from the river, I felt "word flow" return, just like that joyful last turn on a long trail home.

Catherine Nixon Cooke
July 2005

Index

Printed in the United States
37077LVS00002B/7-108